I0482120

Praise for *You're a Leader - Now What?*

"If I had this information years ago I would have out-Donald Donald Trump!"
- C.J. Speros - CEO, The Speros Companies, Phoenix, AZ

"I'd been worrying for years on how to develop a leadership style. This book helped me to develop the path to the type of leader I'd like to be, in one afternoon."
- D. Cueva - MDF Management, Irvine, CA

"WOW, a leadership book that can also be applied to the family. I never found that before!"
- Bill Baar, Phoenix, AZ

"I thought one of the strongest aspects of the book was the several times you gave specific instructions to the reader to do certain things...Such concrete suggestions help bring your points down to earth."
- Geoff Shell - Charter school executive, Tempe, AZ

"...I think most books on leadership are rather dry (good bed time reading). I found your concise approach refreshing."
- D. Erchull - Principal, Global Risk Partners

"This is not just a book. It's a common sense, easily readable, self-contained solution to so many leadership problems."

- J. Schmierbach - Business owner, Marissa, IL

"If there's only one leadership book I can use to refer to and circulate, it's this one...the chapter on Recognition really struck a chord with me. I know that I strive for recognition. I am willing to give 110% when I know there will be a 'good job' at the end of the project. This helps me apply the recognition technique to my direct reports and peers."

- M. Lavin - Electrical engineer, Phoenix, AZ.

"This book is a brief, concise, how to 'play book' of fundamental Leadership principles for the young and aspiring 'want to be' leader as well as the seasoned and successful CEO who wants to stay on top of the game.

The Principles and messages framed are as fundamental to Leadership as the axiom 'You cannot manage what you cannot measure' is to evaluating business performance...It is excellent and very well written.

I especially like your writing style, i.e. an A.B.C., bulleted, 1.,2.,3., and bold highlights where appropriate. This writing approach conveys the maximum message with a minimum of words."

- A. "Butch" Madrazo, Past Chairman and President Silver Fox Advisors, Houston, TX

YOU'RE A LEADER - *Now What?*

Knowing
What
To Do
Next

Len Fuchs
&
John Nicholas

Real Leaders Institute, LLC

Inquiries regarding permission for use of the material contained in this book should be addressed to the publisher:
Real Leaders Institute, LLC
P.O. Box 2557
Gilbert, AZ 85299
USA
Telephone/Fax: 480.219.5509

Gaining The Edge,™
Real Leaders Institute,™
Real Leaders Digest,™
Thoughts While Shaving™

and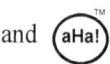

are all trademarks of Real Leaders Institute, LLC

ISBN-10: 1535104015
ISBN-13: 978-1535104012
Library of Congress Control Number 2006940105

Printed in United States of America
10 9 8 7 6 5 4 3 2 1 0

YOU'RE A LEADER - Now What? is dedicated
to all those aspiring to be leaders and those
interested in improving their
leadership skills.

"People ask the difference between a leader and a boss...The leader works in the open and the boss in covert. The leader leads, and the boss drives."

Theodore Roosevelt
President of the United States
1901- 1909

CONTENTS

Special Note

This book was written by two authors. However, you will see "I" occasionally. That's because we worked on certain chapters individually and chose to write those in the first person to express our personal experiences. Whether first person or other, we both agree on the information presented so that you may benefit from this straight forward personal approach.

PREFACE

Why you should read this book

You have picked up this book because of your desire to become a leader or develop your leadership skills or assist your organization in developing leaders. You know that leadership is the key to effectiveness and competitive strength in being successful in whatever endeavors you might pursue. This book is a leadership *"How to"* in ten chapters.

As you read the book, you will discover that leadership lies at the center of every job in your organization and that good leadership lies at the heart of problem solving. By institutionalizing leadership you will go a long way toward increasing your and your fellow employees' leadership abilities.

This book will provide you with the tools required to make leadership part of your everyday process. When you put into practice the principles described in this book, you'll have taken a big step toward becoming a better leader. People in your organization will notice the difference and will follow your lead.

Carl G. Schneider
Maj. Gen. USAF (Ret)

1

DEFINE THE LEADER YOU WANT TO BE

AN ESSENTIAL THREE STEP PROCESS

*E*veryone can stand improvement whether you are a first time supervisor or a CEO or anywhere in between. Often those who don't seek a better way are those who need it most.

In many of the seminars and training sessions I've conducted over the years the most common response has been, *"I wish my boss was here to learn this!"* We can all improve so that the response will be, *"My boss is a good leader and sure does it that way!"*

There are **THREE STEPS** to defining the type of leader you want to be:

1. MAKE YOUR LIST

Take out pen and paper and make a numbered list that answers the statement, *"I respond best to the leader who..."*
Example of a list:

1. *...takes the time to hear me out and focuses on just our discussion.*

2. *...gives clear and concise instructions and then does not micromanage but gets out of the way and let's me do my job.*

3. *...shows appreciation and gives recognition to people on a regular basis for achievement no matter how small.*

4. *...makes an effort to assign interesting challenges and projects that help people to grow.*

5. *...is more of a coach and a counselor than a boss who I'm comfortable enough to go to with any problem or situation.*

6. *...provides support when delegating jobs to me by insuring that everyone involved knows that I have the authority or the backing that goes along with the responsibility.*

7. *...always does the right thing even when it makes him/her unpopular either up or down the line.*

You get the idea. This list could be shorter or longer depending on the thought and effort you put into it.

What you have just done is create a plan to follow that defines the type of leader you want to be. This is your road map that gets you from where you are now to being recognized as a more *effective leader*.

Now, print the list on a piece of paper or 3x5 card(s). Keep it in a place where you have regular access to it. Be sure to include the beginning sentence, *"I respond best to the leader who..."*

Refer to it regularly especially during "blank" times (while waiting in offices, lobbies, airports). <u>By regularly applying them you will begin to develop a leadership edge</u> (even a slight edge can be powerful) that others cannot help but notice.

"Did I do this today?" That's the question you should regularly apply to each of the items on your list. Do not let your list remain static. Keep it dynamic by adding, revising, combining and refining it. Yes, I know it takes effort and no one will be looking over your shoulder or giving you a deadline to submit it. You will have to *discipline* yourself on that. Will the results be worth it? *You bet!*

2. DEVELOP YOUR PHILOSOPHY OF LEADERSHIP

It's not necessary to become the Aristotle of your organization, but it is necessary that you have a leadership credo that you follow consistently. As a young Naval officer I adopted the leadership philosophy of a famous WWII hero, Admiral Arleigh Burke:

1. Know your job

2. Take care of your people

3. Do the right thing

This is the **KISS** principle (*Keep It Simple Stupid*) on steroids. His guidance is applicable to any type of organization. Yes, I revised it slightly to meet current times and different venue (he actually said, *"Take care of your men"*), but the spirit of the philosophy is preserved.

You may run across people in your organization who have a recognized credo that they are not necessarily aware of such as, *"Ready! Fire! Aim!"* (believe it or not sometimes that's a good approach. I don't recommend it for now). What I do recommend is that you develop a consistent approach to good leadership for which you will become recognized.

Let's discuss, *"Know your job."* That may seem so obvious. But, is it? Don't misinterpret that to mean that you must be able to do everything better than your staff, have all the answers, never make a wrong decision and never ask for help because that's a sign of weakness. No, no, no! **Know your job means knowing the broad mission of your area, your specific responsibilities, who can help you get the job done and whether it's done right and in a timely manner.** That's a mouthful, but it covers it.

Does the president of a home building company have to know how to frame a home? Does the captain of a Navy ship have to know how to wind a gyro motor? Does a pilot have to know how to perform a six month overhaul on his aircraft? Not necessarily. **What they must know how to do is set a direction**

and understand what needs to be done to get there and be sure that they have people who are trained in those areas, well taken care of and are recognized for doing their jobs well. Now you begin to see the basis of true leadership.

Here's another example derived from observations of successful leaders: *Try it! Fix it! Do it!* Adopt these philosophies or develop your own, but <u>have one that is practical, realistic and applicable on a consistent basis</u> that others will associate with you.

As for, *"Take care of your people"* I once heard of the *"Treat them like dogs"* approach: walk them, feed them, water them, stroke them, talk to them, sing to them...not literally, of course, but you see the idea. Translate this into:

- **Always be visible and available to your staff.**

- **Insure that they get the proper training.**

- **See to it that they are properly "housed" with a proper work station, equipment, lighting.**

- **Go to bat for them, even if it makes you unpopular with senior management.**

- **Make them feel important by sharing company information that let's them know how you are doing.**

- **Immediately squash rumors by keeping them informed.**

- Post a daily stock quote and progress chart showing your standing toward a goal.
- Take opportunities to celebrate successes, even if they are not work related.

I once had an office staff member who, after I initiated fire extinguisher training for office personnel, came in one morning beaming over an action he took at his apartment complex the night before. A fire erupted in the next door unit. He immediately knew what to do, went into action, pulled the fire extinguisher from the wall, operated it properly, doused the fire and was considered a hero by the other tenants.

We used this as a reason to celebrate in our department; cake, soft drinks and a memo on the bulletin board outlining his heroic action.

Look around, be creative, find reasons to celebrate and let people know you care about them. **Remember, people don't care how much you know, they just want to know how much you care.**

"Do the right thing." That should become your daily mantra. It works both ways. If taking a necessary action makes you unpopular, then so be it. Not taking a necessary action might maintain your popularity with a few malcontents, but in the long run will demoralize the good people in your group. You are the morale officer, like it or not.

The best way to maintain morale is to **immediately be decisive in unpleasant situations, always being fair and even handed.** Also, when you make a mistake - admit it. *"I*

thought I was headed in the right direction, but goofed!"
Staff will rally around a leader who makes an honest mistake and admits it. That sets the example. You can always expect honest feed back when you create that type of atmosphere.

---

3. BE A PERPETUAL STUDENT OF THE HUMAN CONDITION

What does that mean? Never stop learning about people. Example: If you want to achieve your goals find out what the goals are of each member of your staff, whether they be further education, skill development in a certain area or a next level position. <u>Develop a concerted effort to help them reach their goals.</u>

Determine how you can help them. By so doing they will help you. It goes the other way too. Find out the goals of superiors and help them reach those, **PROVIDED** that it does not violate any of the precepts discussed here or interferes with leading your own staff properly.

SUMMARY

1. **Outline** the type of leadership characteristics that motivate you and <u>adopt and adapt them</u>.

2. **Make an effort** to let your staff know you care by <u>showing them through actions.</u>

3. **Take opportunities**, no matter how small, to <u>celebrate successes.</u>

4. Try to understand people from their perspective rather than try to force them into being your clone.

5. Review this material several times until it becomes ingrained. Practice the steps outlined here. You might be surprised what it will do for your confidence AND how others will begin to recognize your good leadership.

 *Face-to-Face!*

2

RECOGNITION IS A BIG DEAL!

"I can live for two weeks on a good compliment."
- Mark Twain

KNOW HOW TO GIVE IT AND GET IT

Surveys have been conducted over the years as to what motivates employees. The major factor that has consistently ranked toward the top, if not at the top, has been:

RECOGNITION

For centuries military organizations around the world have understood that medals have been a major motivating factor in heroic performance. Napoleon is credited with having said that men will risk their lives for a few colorful ribbons. During the American Civil War the Union Army's Red Badge of Courage was a coveted and sought after form of recognition.

What are the forms of recognition that can be given in private sector organizations today that motivate employees to top performance? Our focus here is not for the entire organization as many have annual awards banquets and events for that purpose. There is also special employee of the month recognitions that many organizations have.

The purpose of this chapter is to supplement those by focusing more on the day to day and nearer term regular needs of people to be recognized and ways to approach recognition from that perspective. **The basic premise here is that people who feel appreciated are the most productive performers. Don't always wait for some long term special event for that. Do it regularly.**

It's important to note at this point a caveat in recognizing people: Always remain within the guidelines approved by your organization. They can and do vary. There are some excellent books on the subject of employee recognition. However, not all methods are universally accepted. Stay within the parameters set by your organization and enjoy the benefits. We will focus on simple, creative, effective ways that should most certainly be almost universally acceptable.

Is money the only motivating force?

Many mangers believe that using money as a reward is all the recognition employees require. When management primarily expresses thanks with cash it send a message to workers that unless they get more cash, their contribution isn't important. The reality is that employees thrive, are motivated and stay with an organization because **their performance is recognized in many different ways.** When given a choice, **workers usually don't rate money at the top of the list of ways to be recognized.** They usually rate genuine **recognition** and **appreciation** at the top. Instead of saying *"good job"* (the way you say *"good morning"*) when catching someone doing great work, they would more appreciate something such as:

> *"This report is superb. I'm going to send it to top management to let them see the great work you're doing for the company."*

That is a compliment that can make any individual feel great for a long time. Look around your organization. You'll be amazed at all the opportunity there is to give recognition.

Most organizations have programs to recognize outstanding performance, but few do it well. Finding creative ways to recognize a job well done is a huge challenge.

GIVING RECOGNITION

If you start by recognizing and rewarding exceptional performance it will tend to be repeated. When other employees **see** what is being recognized they will follow suit. Here are **five areas** of when and what to *recognize* and *celebrate*:

1. Catch people in the act of doing something good

Give *recognition* immediately and, when appropriate, *celebrate*. This gives immediate reinforcement to the individual and is an example to motivate others to better performance. **Take every opportunity to have a cake and**

cookies celebration to specifically recognize a person for some exceptional performance. As corny as this may sound it's very effective. Leave the cake and cookies on the table so they may be accessed throughout the day. Invite other departments or groups to participate. Leave a small sign on the table announcing the reason for the celebration. It sends the message, *"I care."*

---

2. Show appreciation of work well done, expressed directly by managers personally or publicly

---

Examples:

- Where possible, have the most senior person in the organization personally recognize the individual by presenting a letter of commendation. If significant enough, have the letter framed and present it at a cake and cookies ceremony or special luncheon.

- If you have a company newsletter, take a picture of the presentation and submit it.

- In any event put a print of the picture on your bulletin board. Do this at least on a quarterly basis. This gives team members something to strive for and can translate into better performance.

---

3. Use testimonials received from customers or other employees as a basis for recognition

---

Testimonials are excellent evidence of an employee's performance. Use every opportunity to broadcast these such as:

- Place the testimonial letter on a bulletin board.
- Send an email to all employees announcing it.
- Read it when you have a meeting.
- Make it a big deal, because it is!

4. Acknowledge achievements

Examples:
- Promotions
- Longevity (with the organization and/or department)
- Academic accomplishments (including any special company training completed)
- Family graduations
- New babies
- Anniversaries
- Birthdays
- Charity work
- Whatever else is worthy of special recognition

Recognize these achievements in front of the individual's peers. (Remember: Recognition does not have to do with just job performance alone.)

5. Have victory celebrations

Make the recognition memorable. This applies to your entire staff. When a certain goal has been reached that required everyone's efforts, reward the entire staff. Here are two examples, both of which can be done between the hours of 11:00 a.m. - 2 p.m.

- If there is a nearby miniature golf course take everyone. If it has a restaurant, or at a nearby restaurant, have a luncheon to congratulate the team. Then go on the "links."

- Offer a small prize to the winner or split up into teams and offer a small plastic trophy to each member of the winning team. Encourage them to display it on their desk.

- Another choice is going to a nearby park that has facilities for a cookout:

    - Designate certain team members to buy hot dogs and hamburgers and all the picnic stuff that goes with it.

    - Meet at a designated area.

    - Give your people an opportunity to demonstrate their organizational and cook-out skills.

    - Enjoy the camaraderie and relaxed conver-sation.

    - Take a frisbee, play volleyball, be creative.

- Designate, in advance, one of the team to write a humorous poem about the group and have them read it aloud.
- Take a walk around the park as a group and enjoy the surroundings together.

You will be surprised how this type of recognition develops bonds and increases the morale and productivity of your team.

In all cases be sure to clear this and get approval for the expenditure. If this is new to your organization, sell them on the idea and be a ground breaker. The results will be worth it because I have practiced both of these type events and **they work**.

"But," you might retort, *"Aren't you taking away time from the job?"* Ok, everyone usually gets an hour for lunch, so you are taking away two additional hours once a quarter. However, I assure you that the increase in morale of your crew will also result in an increase in productivity that will more than make up for those two extra hours.

There may be some who must stay behind in a "duty status" to maintain certain necessary functions. Make it up to them someway such as early off. Set up an alternating schedule for the next event. Be creative and fair. That's what leadership is all about.

DON'TS

1. Don't recognize everyone equally for different

levels of achievement. If you reward everyone equally your high performers will resent the low performers getting the same recognition. Eventually your high performers may look for a job elsewhere where their talents may be better recognized.

2. **Don't reprimand in public.** Always reprimand **in private.** No one likes to be ridiculed in front of others. An effective way to reprimand is calmly, in a mentoring way over a meal. Send out for sandwiches and have a closed door session. This creates a non-threatening environment in which to get agreement on a game plan for improvement including a follow-up evaluation.

GETTING RECOGNITION

Actively seeking recognition in your work group can be done without being branded a "suck-up" or blowing your own horn. Here are two techniques:

1. **Share recognition with others for their efforts in anything where you stand to gain the full recognition.** People (including bosses) notice those who treat others with this type of respect.

> *By sharing recognition with others you will be recognized as a caring individual who does not go out and grab full glory on the backs of others.*

Your peers and bosses do realize where the credit should be given. You'll elevate your status in their eyes far more this way than grabbing for the whole "enchilada." By *giving* you'll also be *getting*.

2. **Another technique in getting recognition is keeping track of your accomplishments on a monthly basis.** In some organizations, when it comes time for annual evaluations, it's generally not based on what you've accomplished during the past year, but more likely what your supervisor remembers that you did during the previous week. In situations such as that does the phrase, *"How quickly they forget!"* mean anything to you?

The way to overcome this and get the full recognition you deserve is to create a regular list of goals and accomplishments for each month and submit it to your manager. Here's how to do that:

1. **Prepare two lists each month.** One list should be titled *Planned Accomplishments for Month of_____* and the next should be titled *Completed Accomplishments & Status Report for Month of_____*.

2. **Make two copies of each.** Keep one for your file and give the other to your manager. Try to keep the list concise and include only those things that generally go beyond what is expected of you on a regular basis. The list should be a minimum of three items and maxi-

mum of seven. That's realistic. If you try to pad it, it will not be well received. The list should always be realistic, sincere and appropriate. Double space between items to be accomplished (you'll see why in the example of the *Completed Accomplishments & Status Report*). Examples (note double spacing between items):

Planned Accomplishments for Month of June 2006

1. Complete training program for new hires within department.

2. Write an article for company newsletter on our new team quality control program.

3. Revise the section on Order Entry for the Systems & Procedures Manual.

The **Planned Accomplishments** report then becomes your **Completed Accomplishments & Status Report** at the end of that month. If the item was completed, then so state. If not, then include the status, such as: **Pending, est. completion mid July 2006.** Here's what the above example of a **Planned Accomplishments for Month of June 2006** report may turn into at the end of that month (enter the status in the double space area you left below the item):

> *Completed Accomplishments & Status Report Month of*
> *June 2006*
>   *1. Complete training program for new hires*
>   *within department.*
>   **In progress, est. completion mid July**
>   **2006**
>   *2. Write an article for company newsletter on*
>   *our new team quality control program.*
>   **Completed**
>   *3. Revise the section on Order Entry for the*
>   *Systems & Procedures Manual.*
>   **Completed**

(The expectation is that you will create these reports in a word processing program and save the reports in a file. When the time comes, just revise the "Planned" report heading in accordance with this example and print it.)

Carry over uncompleted items into the next month always giving a status and estimated completion date. Meet with your manager on a regular basis and discuss the list of accomplishments and goals you've achieved. Include the goals you've set for the next month and how you plan on achieving them. Now, the next time your evaluation is due it will be easier for your evaluator to give you the recognition you truly have earned and deserve because your achievements have been documented and archived. Does this require discipline and effort on your part? You bet! Is it worth it? You bet, in spades! Why? It's a method that prompts you to set and accomplish goals on a regular basis that you might not otherwise do and you'll see rewards you might not otherwise get.

Some *real world* discussion:
There may be instances where your manager may not wish to meet with you because of time constraints. Your manager may even tell you it's not necessary to submit a monthly report. In that case, let your manager know you're doing it anyway and it's no additional trouble to make an extra copy.

> **In any event always submit a folder of copies of your reports at evaluation time as a refresher for your manager.** You may be surprised to find how many of your items will appear verbatim on your evaluations under *goals and accomplishments.*

The old saying, *"What's good for the goose is good for the gander"* also applies here. For those who report to you, have them do the same type reports. It will also make your giving them formal evaluations that much easier and accurate. This will also help them to grow. It acts as a motivator for others to seek out items "above and beyond" to accomplish. That, in and of itself, can lead to better performance.

CONCLUSION

Giving and getting recognition is not difficult. It does take work and effort, but in the long run **elevates both the giver and getter.** Now that you know some of the secrets and techniques, go forth and *recognize* and *be recognized.*

(aHa!) *Respect is where it's at!*

3

THE 7 GREATEST MISTAKES LEADERS MAKE & HOW TO AVOID THEM

"You must learn from the mistakes of others. You can't possibly live long enough to make them all yourself."

- Sam Levinson

KNOW THE PITFALLS

*T*his chapter will be presented in the form of an interview between the authors. John Nicholas (**J**), will be asking Len Fuchs (**L**), questions about his experiences and observations of the major mistakes leaders make and how to avoid them.

J - Len, with your extensive leadership experience in the Marine Corps, the corporate world and as an entrepreneur, what have you observed as the greatest mistakes leaders make?

L - Well, John, you're right I have observed some rather blatant mistakes that otherwise good leaders make regularly that prevents them from realizing their full potential. It's easy to make mistakes as a leader. The real talent is in recognizing mistakes before they become disastrous and you become a flash-in-the-pan spectacular failure.

The greatest mistakes leaders make are very ego-centered. As a result the leader is usually the last to recognize that there is anything wrong. We can all improve. Therefore, the first step toward that process is to recognize that you're making the same mistake over and over expecting different results.

J - Isn't that the definition of INSANITY?

L - Absolutely! But, don't get ahead of me. I'm still on the question of mistakes. I've thought about this for a long time and have counseled others on it. This is the first time I've collated, organized and crystallized the mistakes for our readers so that they have some guidelines to follow.

I could probably come up with 10 or even a dozen and call them the *Ten Broken Commandments of Leadership* or the *Dirty Dozen Mistakes Leaders Make.* However, for our purposes let's focus on the 7 greatest mistakes that would definitely be included in each of those.

I must clarify that not all leaders suffer from these maladies. But, if you have just one, that's one too many. So, pay attention because the number one mistake is:

**1. TRYING TO DOMINATE THE ORGANI-
ZATION or the "ME ONLY SYNDROME"**

That is the most ego-centered pitfall of those with otherwise good leadership potential.

J - Wait a minute, Len! Aren't leaders supposed to be aggressive and ambitious?

L - Yes, but within a self controlled context. All to often they vastly overestimate the extent to which they actually control events and vastly underestimate the role of chance and circumstances in their success.

Successful leaders try to shape the future precisely because they know that they can't dominate it. Another symptom of leaders who suffer from illusion of personal preeminence is that they tend to see people as material to be molded, or as audiences for their performances. They have a tendency to favor those who "suck up" to them.

J - That doesn't sound good. In fact, it smacks of excessive ego. But, isn't some ego healthy?

L - Some ego is healthy, but not when it leads to the "ME ONLY SYNDROME." We should keep going back to

Willy Shakespeare and his advice, *"To thine own self be true."* That applies in so many areas of leadership and especially here. Learn to be honest and objective about yourself.

J - Isn't it part of the human condition that we want to be recognized and rewarded for good performance?

L - Of course, leaders want to be recognized and rewarded for their efforts and accomplishments. But, some are far too occupied with *themselves.* Those are leaders whose overriding concerns are how much credit they're getting, how much money they're making and how fast they're advancing.

They are the type who fail to reward or praise individuals in front of others because, as the leader, they feel the glory should be all theirs, all the time. They have focused their ambition on themselves rather than the organization or on others. Big mistake!

J - Isn't there a favorite cartoon you have that zeroes in on that?

L - Yes, it pictures a man sitting behind a large desk holding a report and talking to a younger person. He's saying, *"I like what you've done here, Tim. That's why I'll enjoy taking credit for it."*

J - It would almost be funny if it wasn't so true?

L - More poignant than funny because it's so rampant in organizations today. At least the boss in the cartoon admits what he's up to. Many don't.

J - What advice would you give leaders on how to avoid the "me only syndrome"?

L - Everyone has something to offer. In order to bring out the best you must create an environment of recognition rather than uncertainty or fear. Employees must feel comfortable enough to speak up freely.

Seek out their ideas. Always listen with the attitude that people who are more directly involved in an area usually have the best insights for how to improve it. Who knows better than those dealing directly with the customer, process or product on a regular basis? You'll be amazed at what you can learn that helps the decision making or planning process. And, at the risk of sounding like a broken record, always give the deserving person the credit up front.

J - You really emphasize this "mistake" and put it at number one. Why is that?

L - Because, for those who are afflicted with it, it's the biggest stumbling block toward long term success. It is the major barrier to overcoming all other mistakes. Unless you overcome this one you'll never overcome the others.

J - What are some of the others?

L - Another mistake is:

---

2. THE INABILITY TO GET ALONG WITH OTHERS

J - To what do you attribute that?

L - Poor interpersonal skills and not caring or even making an effort to get along. You expect others to make the effort to get along with you. This is one of the single biggest reasons for failure - especially in the early and middle stages of a leader's career. It's also the most crucial flaw to recognize and remedy.

J - Why is that?

L - The individual believes that if people aren't coming with their problems then everything must be going well. The reality is that their anti-social behavior coupled with their *"I don't care"* attitude creates a barrier. That's why they will never gain loyalty or knowledge of what's really happening.

For example, every good military leader knows that when their troops stop coming to them with their problems, they've lost control. The same is true of private sector organizations.

J - Isn't control an important part of leadership?

L- Indeed it is, but within a broad context. No one can maintain control in an organization unless they are kept up-dated as events unfold. If you create a *"shoot-the-messenger"* atmosphere you'll find out what's happening only when it's too late to salvage the situation.

J - What's the best way to avoid this and stay in control?

L - The best way to maintain control is to appreciate that the people in your organization don't care how much you know, but want to know how much you care. When you create a caring environment you'll be kept in the loop, will know what's going on and have time to be more proactive rather than reactive.

J - That certainly makes sense. But, aren't some leaders just naturally predisposed to achieving goals without the need for much input?

L - That's like playing Russian roulette, you'll win a few times, but the law of averages will eventually catch up and then BANG! Never play that dangerous game with your life and career. Do what has proven to work well consistently. Avoid trying to run between the rain drops because you feel you can dodge it all. That leads to underestimating obstacles.

J - Don't tell me! That's the next greatest mistake leaders make, isn't it?

L - Aha! You're paying attention. Yes, the next greatest mistake leaders make is:

> **3. UNDERESTIMATING OBSTACLES**

J - How does that happen?

L - Leaders sometimes become so enamored with what they want to achieve that they often overlook or underestimate the difficulty of actually achieving particular goals. When that happens, it often becomes impossible for a leader to recognize when an escalating commitment is getting out of hand.

J - I've seen that. Isn't that one of the main reasons that a leader doesn't want to become associated with a losing project they started?

L - Good observation! As a result they will keep throwing more money, resources and personnel at the problem until it becomes too difficult and almost impossible to change direction.

J - When a project is headed south, what do you suggest?

L - Remember and apply the old saying, *"First loss is best loss."* Admit the mistake and move on.

J - **As an example of that advice I once heard a leader say, *"It's not the first time I've thrown money down a rat hole."***

L - What is your opinion of that leader?

J - **Great respect!**

L - I rest my case.

J - **Don't some leaders stick with a direction because they were able to overcome obstacles in the same way in the past?**

L - Unfortunately for them and their organization, that's true. By so doing they engineer themselves into the next truly great mistake:

---

4. STUBBORNLY RELYING ON WHAT WORKED IN THE PAST AND FAILING TO ADAPT TO NEWER AND BETTER WAYS

J - **Wow! That's a mouthful! Would you explain how that boomerangs against them?**

L - The inability to adapt to change is the fatal flaw of the fast-tracker. They cling to a once successful management or business strategy long after it stops producing results. Those type leaders accelerate their organization's decline by reverting to what they regard as tried and true strategies they developed.

Some leaders fail to consider innovations other than those that made their organization successful in the past. They develop tunnel vision and ignore any outside innovation sources.

The problem is: That type leader had one extraordinary success in the past that became, in their mind, a universal one size fits all strategy forever. Then they let themselves be defined by that success the rest of their career. Eventually they fail because they learned one particular lesson too well.

J - **Would you say they operate in a state of arrested development?**

L - Couldn't have said it better. Add to that the **NIH** (**N**ot **I**nvented **H**ere) attitude along with, *"That's the way we've always done it"* and you begin to see why some organizations are headed toward the iceberg.

J - **What are some examples of companies that have gone that route?**

L - I won't name specific companies, but will give these examples: Over the past 15 years over half of the 30 companies that comprise the *Dow Industrial Averages* have been replaced by more progressive and successful companies. Another example is the recording industry. Any company that stubbornly stayed in the vinyl record pressing business is not doing too well today, even though I understand there is still some of that going on.

J - But, not much.

L - You said it. Either continue to seek out newer and better ways, adapt and change with the times or get mired in the ooze of obsolescence.

J - Can I quote you on that?

L - You can!

J - I bet we could make a great poster with that saying that would certainly get the message across.

L - Speaking of getting messages across, that brings us to the next greatest mistake:

> **5. DELIVERING A CONFUSING MESSAGE**

I've often observed that leaders, instead of making their messages simple and direct, confuse people with needless complexity. They forget, or are unaware of the

KISS principle of communications (**K**eep **I**t **S**imple **S**tupid).

J - Ahhh, the big "C" communication. Are we going to cover that now?

L - We'll just touch on it because that, in and of itself, is a whole major topic. You don't have to be a great orator or public speaker to be a good communicator. You do have to be clear and concise.

Good communicators don't hide behind emails and memos. They make time for face time. Being the talker all the time does not make you a good communicator. Being a good listener and taking time to listen is part of being a good communicator.

J - Why is listening part of good communications?

L - Making the other party feel they have your undivided attention is imperative to good communications. It sends out the message that they are important enough to command your attention.

Many companies labor over mission statements that express the importance of its people. Then, some of its leaders send out a different message by doing unrelated things while the other party is speaking. That's one of the worst and most confusing messages you can send because it says, *"You aren't important and neither is anything you have to say."* That will rarely lead to peak performance and loyalty.

J - I see. What other facets are there of good communications?

L - Having a sense of humor is part of being a good communicator. Examples abound of presidents Lincoln and Reagan and their excellent abilities to reduce complicated situations to just a few simple statements, often humorous ones. Many famous quotations are barely two lines long, but what was said made an impact.

Communicators are motivators. It's one thing to order someone to do something, but it's quite another to get them to do it on their own as though it was their own idea. The best communicators always show respect for their audience and try to get them to "buy into" whatever they are proposing.

Good leaders know that people will support what they help to create. So, include them in the process by giving them a voice and listening ear. Good leaders also know that motivated people always turn in the best performances.

J - Speaking of performances, how should a leader handle set backs in theirs?

L - Interesting that you should bring that up because it ties right in with the next major mistake leaders make:

6. FAILURE TO REBOUND

J - What's the reason for that?

L - Probably embarrassment and a lot of ego. Those who don't rebound well tend to react to failure by becoming defensive. They try to conceal it, minimize it or blame circumstances and others.

Those leaders who lapse into denial and don't or won't learn the lessons from their failures are doomed to repeat them. Sometimes they may even recede into the background and become fearful of accepting future responsibilities.

Fear of failure can be debilitating. There's an old equestrian axiom that the best way to overcome the fear of horseback riding when you've fallen off is to immediately get back on the horse. Nuff said.

J - Is "getting back on the horse" the best reaction to failure?

L - That's what I've observed. In contrast to those who don't rebound, successful leaders admit where they have erred and try to learn from their mistakes. Since most careers zigzag, the ability to handle set backs and failures well can make or break a climb to higher levels.

On his 400th attempt to invent a light bulb, Thomas

Edison was asked by a reporter what it felt like to be a failure. Edison replied that he wasn't a failure, but had learned 400 ways how not to make a light bulb. In other words learn from mistakes and what doesn't work so you can focus direction toward what may work. It's called experience and there's no substitute for it. It led to the successful light bulb and many other great inventions, I might add.

We all know of people who have succeeded after failures. I sometimes feel that a few failures are a necessary prerequisite to success. It's not the failures so much as how you react to them and what you learn from them. You must be confident enough to admit them openly and move forward.

J - So, "fess up," learn from the experience and move forward.

L - You got it!

J - Earlier you said there were 7 greatest mistakes leaders make. We've covered six. What's the final one?

L - This is a tough one, but I've seen the effects of this one too often not to include it in the list. It's:

---

7. ELIMINATING THOSE NOT BLINDLY 100% BEHIND THEM

As I said, this is a tough one and needs explaining. Every leader wants and needs support. However, it should not be at the expense of creating an environment of fear of elimination and retribution for those not immediately, without question, 100% behind their program. There should be room for opposing ideas.

That type of leader goes forth with the banner that anyone who doesn't blindly rally to the cause is undermining the organization. They attempt to surround themselves with "clones" in order to maintain loyalty to the cause. People should not be in fear to tell the emporer he has no clothes.

J - Well, isn't loyalty important?

L - Blind following is not loyalty! In an organization such as that, hesitant individuals, with good reason to be so, are given a choice: Get with the plan or leave.

Leaders who try to stifle dissent only drive it underground. When this happens the organization eventually declines. Dictatorial organizations, whether they be teams, departments, branches, divisions or a whole corporate structure are headed for disaster when there's no one left who feels free enough to voice a warning.

This leads to telling outsiders what's wrong because the insiders won't listen. There have been a few examples of this on the news from Wall Street. The Enron debacle of a few year ago is an excellent example of that.

J - So, a good leader should have the boldness to tell the emperor when he has no clothes.

L - Yes, but in a tactful manner and, when possible, with some well thought out alternatives.

J - Are you saying that a leader shouldn't have strong views and should lead by consensus only?

L - That's an oversimplification. A good leader should seek other opinions, even contrary ones and take them to heart. However, he must ultimately make the decision based on all of the facts and opinions presented. A leader should not work in a vacuum.

I must add that this excludes life and death situations often found in the military where there's no time for a meeting of the minds. However, few if any situations in non-military organizations have that type of environment. When you have time and advisors, use them.

You can still have strong views yet still listen to the views of others. That's different than continually turning a deaf ear with the attitude that no one else has a better idea.

Our great country was built on the principle of freedom to dissent. Once you take that away you lose the benefits of the process. As a point of clarification: Once a decision has been reached through the process of open discussion, debate and dissent, without fear of retribution and the decision is ethical, then it's incumbent on the people in an organization to support it. You have a responsibility of setting the example at your level for others to see.

J - Kind of like, "Do as I say AND do as I do."

L - A tough challenge, but right on the money. A well run organization with leaders who have purged themselves of the mistakes outlined here can bank on their people for this support. That leads to overall success.

J - I'm going to summarize the 7 greatest mistakes:

SUMMARY

1. TRYING TO DOMINATE THE ORGANIZATION or the *"ME ONLY SYNDROME"*

2. THE INABILITY TO GET ALONG WITH OTHERS

3. UNDERESTIMATING OBSTACLES

4. STUBBORNLY RELYING ON WHAT WORKED IN THE PAST AND FAILING TO ADAPT TO NEWER AND BETTER WAYS

5. DELIVERING A CONFUSING MESSAGE

6. FAILURE TO REBOUND

7. ELIMINATING THOSE NOT BLINDLY 100% BEHIND THEM

L - That summarizes the list.

J - **How does someone recognize that they make any of these mistakes and once they do how do you suggest they correct them?**

L - This may seem an oversimplification but it works. Have a trusted friend or mentor evaluate whether you exhibit any of the mistakes outlined here, even to some small degree. If you're really feeling adventurous, ask your spouse or significant other. Be confident enough to accept constructive criticism, without becoming defensive or trying to justify your actions or inactions as the case may be.

J - **Isn't that one of the hardest things for a leader to do when others look to them for answers?**

L - When leaders feel they have all the answers, they have no way to learn from new answers. That may well be the biggest mistake. First, no one has all the answers. Trying to convey that image will inevitably work against you. There's nothing wrong with saying, "I don't know," provided that you take steps to find out or delegate someone to do so. If you do, be certain to give them credit up front.

J - **Len, thanks for sharing your observations and expe-**

rience. They certainly should help anyone seeking to become a better leader. Is there any parting advice you would give?

L - Sure, John, it's a consistent mantra: *TRY IT! FIX IT! DO IT!*

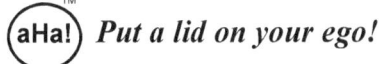 *Put a lid on your ego!*

4

HOW TO DELEGATE
EFFECTIVELY

(There are some differences between leading and managing, which is a whole other subject. For the purposes of this chapter on DELEGATING, the terms "leaders" and "managers" will be used synonymously.)

IT'S A MULTI-STEP PROCESS

*A*ll you have to do is order a subordinate to do something and expect that it will be done properly and in a timely manner. Right? Not so fast! Unfortunately, that is the way some managers treat delegation. They then put the full blame on the other party for inadequate performance or missed deadlines. There is a difference between giving orders and delegating effectively.

DELEGATING IS A TWO WAY STREET

One of the most comprehensive definitions I've come across that emphasizes this is by Stephanie Wilson, author of, *The Organized Executive*:

"It's entrusting the matter to the other person. It involves mutual commitment. The person to whom you are delegating makes a commitment to meet your expectations. For you it means a commitment to give staff full cooperation, backing, recognition."

All too often leaders find that *"entrusting"* is very difficult. Robert B. Nelson, in his book, *Delegation*, lists these **five most typical excuses** managers give for not delegating:

1. My staff lacks the experience.

2. It takes more time to explain than to do the job myself.

3. A mistake by an employee can be costly.

4. I'm concerned about lack of control over their performance.

5. My position enables me to get quicker action.

Do any of these sound familiar? All of these boils down to the most common reason for failure to delegate:

INSECURITY

Balance the **benefits** against the excuses:
- **Mobilize resources**
- **You will focus on doing your own tasks better**
- **Increase your leadership potential**
- **More time for managerial actions**
- **Your company becomes better and more profitable**

What is required to increase your delegating skills? Effective delegating requires good communication skills. Successful delegation takes practice and effort to master. In addition to the benefits listed above it accomplishes **two significant factors**:

> **1. You will end up with more time that helps you to achieve much more when you don't try to do everything yourself.**
>
> **2. It gives your staff more opportunity to grow.**

Effective delegating is a **SIX STEP** process. Here are the steps, in sequential order, that will help you become successful at *delegation*:

1. ESTABLISH THE GOAL

- **Determine the task to be delegated.** Don't be ambiguous. Describe the task and the goal you're trying to accomplish. That's the first most critical step in effective delegation.

- **Communicate the task clearly.** Clarify what part they are playing in the overall picture and the importance and benefits of their role. (Yes, this may require some *"selling"* on your part.)

- **Use words that are easily understood.** If the project is detailed and involved, then write out the basic guidelines so the employee can recheck them to be sure they are on the right track.

- **Delegate responsibility, not drudge work.** Too many managers confuse delegating responsibility with dumping undesirable work on someone. Delegate the entire task, not just those parts you wish to avoid. Employees know the difference, not to mention the effects on your reputation as a leader.

2. SET EXPECTATIONS

- **Outline the standards** you expect to be followed.

- **Indicate what you will do to assist** and what you expect to be done independently.

- **Don't delegate a project and then insist that the employee do it your way,** with no room for personal initiative.

- **Listen to ideas.** Let the individual put their own spin on the assignment. They may actually have a better way.

- **Match the task to the person.** Try to delegate assignments that will capitalize on the person's talents and interests. Build the employee's confidence by assigning low risk projects first.

- **Establish the accountability required.**

3. SET DEADLINES

- **Set a due date.** This is mandatory. Too many projects fail because due dates are not viewed as compulsory. When assigning a due date explain how this assignment relates to other priorities.

- **A goal is just a wish until you assign a time limit.**
- There may be multiple time limits for various phases of projects you are delegating. **Make sure these are understood.**

---

4. SET REFERENCE POINTS

- **Set reference points along the way** through required reports in order to know that you are on track, within time frames and making progress.

- **Track the progress.** As the deadline nears, check to make sure that everything is on target and if additional support is needed.

---

5. PROVIDE SUPPORT

- **It is vital to give the authority needed** to accomplish the goal and fulfill the responsibility. Few things are more frustrating than to be given a responsibility without the authority to get the job done. Avoid being that type of leader.

- **Provide support by notifying other** managers,

departments and functions both inside and outside of your area of control who would be involved.

- **Make clear that the person represents you** and that the same cooperation should be given them as you in the fulfillment of the mission. It's advisable to do it in **writing or by personal visit, with the staff member present.**

- **Support includes providing resources:**
  - If secretarial help is necessary, then arrange for it.

  - If personal vehicle travel is necessary, then make arrangements for reimbursement. Avoid putting the person in a position to have to ask. **Never make a *"beggar"* out of anyone** on your staff for anything you should foresee as fair recompense. (Remember the second part of the leadership philosophy from Chapter 1: *"Take care of your people."*)

  - **It includes coaching along the way.** Don't be tempted to take over the project if you see it waning. The person performing the task may not do it as well as you would. Nevertheless, weigh the time you might lose against the time you'll save in the long run by the experience they will gain.

6. DEBRIEF and EVALUATE

- The U.S. military established **debriefing and evaluating** as standard operating procedure after a mission is completed. It works well and is well worth adopting and adapting. The reason is that it answers what went right, what went wrong and the reasons for both. This information is then used to revise, modify and otherwise fine-tune future operational procedures to establish the most effective standards.

- A good way to apply this system is to have the person ask themselves and answer the question: *"If I had it to do over again, what would I do the same, what would I do differently and why?"*

- This is an excellent opportunity to evaluate the performance rather than wait for an annual review. **Compliment where appropriate and critique, coach and counsel where necessary.** This helps growth, confidence and loyalty.

Once you understand the process of effective delegation, the challenge then becomes applying it to the right people. Who are the right people? **ACHIEVERS!** You can *identify* **ACHIEVERS** as those who seek:

- **Recognition**
- **Challenges**
- **Rewards**
- **Satisfaction**
- **Training**

When you've identified those people you can begin to apply the process. Following are two "scenarios" to apply this information to be able to see **HOW** it works:

> **Delegating Scenario Case #1**

You **Delegate** responsibility to a staff member to begin completing a weekly report that previously you handled solely yourself. It formed the basis of a regular report that you gave at a weekly senior staff meeting.

Vital information must come from the accounting department (of which you are not part). Because of your position you were always able to obtain this information to complete the report on time.

Now the accounting department won't give the information to your staff member in a timely manner. As a result, your staff member feels frustrated because of lack of authority, yet having the responsibility to get the report to you on time.

How would you handle that situation?

Take some time to think this through and then determine how you would have applied the **Six Steps of Effective Delegation.** See how you would have responded to the questions under each step:

Step 1. Establish The Goal

- Did you determine that you would brief your staff member on the <u>importance of the information in the report</u> and how it forms a piece of the big picture that is vital to the on-going operation of the company?

- Did you further point out that it was <u>so important that you handled it solely yourself</u> in the past?

- Did you indicate the trust you had in the staff member that they could complete the report for you and, <u>as a result, increase their knowledge and worth to you and the organization?</u>

Step 2. Set Expectations
- Did you <u>set the standards</u> of the report by showing copies of past reports and the need for accuracy and clarity?

- Did you ask for <u>ideas to help improve the report,</u> consolidate information through easy to see and understand graphs and charts (but, run these by you first before any changes were implemented)?

- Did you make the <u>priority</u> over other responsibilities clear and which took precedent?

- Did you establish what you expected them to do <u>independently</u> and what should be <u>reviewed with you</u> during the process?

- Did you let them know what they can expect in support from you to facilitate obtaining information from other departments and secretarial help in compiling the report?

Step 3. Set Deadlines
- Did you set a deadline of when you needed a <u>rough draft</u> for your input and to be sure it is progressing properly?
- Did you set the deadline of when you needed the <u>completed report</u> on your desk?

Step 4. Set Reference Points
- In this scenario this step coincides with Step 3. It becomes more relevant the longer and more involved the report or project. In that case, progress reports at <u>certain points along the way</u> would be advisable.

Step 5. Provide Support
- Did you meet with or notify, in writing, the accounting department head that this staff member has been given this new responsibility and represents you in obtaining the subject data?
- Did you <u>notify others</u> in your department as to this <u>new responsibility</u> and its <u>priority</u>?
- Did you make certain that secretarial staff was <u>aware of the importance</u> of the report and the <u>precedent</u> it would take over any routine items?

Step 6. Debrief & Evaluate
- Did you indicate that there would be a <u>debriefing</u>

session after the first rough draft and the first completed report and the reasons why?

- Did you make it clear that this is a two-way session in which you would be open to ways to improve the process, determine the cooperation the staff member received and where help and support would be appropriate?

- Did you set a time frame where a more formal evaluation of the performance would be done, such as, after 30 days (approximately four reports)?

If you can answer all of these satisfactorily, then kudos to your application of the true **Delegation** process. These are, by no means, the only approaches. They do form the basis for **HOW** to get good results. The sequence shown is typical and could vary. However, only the first and last steps should always be in the sequence shown. The middle steps do not necessarily have to follow the sequence presented here. Their sequence can be altered to fit the situation.

By approaching **Delegation** on the basis of this **Six Step** process you will see an improvement in staff performance, your own performance, morale and respect for how you treat and support your staff and fellow workers.

Delegating Scenario Case #2

(This Case involves a field process in a volume home building sit-uation. However, it could be applied to almost any business situa-

tion from manufacturing a product to developing software. Just substitute terms such as "supervisor" or "supplier" or "products" where appropriate.)

You have a framing subcontractor who has begun to make some obvious errors lately. You have too many homes under construction to be able to supervise as carefully as you would like. Also, you have an unexpected priority assignment that you are required to do.

It's Monday and you must have ten homes framed and inspection ready by the end of the day on Friday. You have no time to do this fully yourself. It's important that these homes meet a specific schedule to eventually be ready for closing in order to meet a quarterly goal. Therefore, it is essential that this progress be made to meet the target deadline. Meanwhile, you must complete that unrelated priority assignment.

What steps would you take in DELEGATING this to "Mike" your assistant?

Before reading the recommended quoted scenario responses outlined below, take a few moments to think of how you would approach this. Do this on an interactive basis by <u>rehearsing</u> in your mind what you would say. Then, see how close you came to the recommendations.

The delegation steps subheadings will not be shown in this scenario. Here's the challenge: See if you can identify the **Six Steps** in the recommended approach and how close you came to a similar approach. Keep in mind there is rarely only one "best way." If you applied the middle steps in a little different sequence, but feel the results would have been the same, that's great!

Recommended Approach
"Mike, ABC Framing has been making a lot of errors lately. They need closer supervision to get them back on track or we won't meet our schedule. That will back up others causing us to miss our business plan for the quarter.

We must have lots 1 - 10 framed and inspection ready by Friday. I won't be able to spend the time I normally do because of another project that will take most of my time and attention. It's important that we become proactive on this now rather than have to scramble later. I need your help.

I'll expect you to take charge immediately. See where we are and what needs to be done. Set up a schedule to insure those homes are complete by the deadline. You'll have to supervise closely to be sure they meet our standards and are correct according to plans.

This is a great opportunity for you to gain experience to help you get to the next level. I may not be readily available at times. That's why I'm counting on you to do the right thing. I know you can do it. If you run into a problem you're not sure of, contact me, but have some solid recommendations for me. Don't just ask me what to do. That's the only way you're going to get ahead.

Right now we're going to meet with ABC's field boss and walk the lots. I'm going to let him know that you're now the final authority on those lots. During the walk, I'll also let the other superintendents know that you have this new responsibility, that you have my full support and to give you full cooperation.

Make a note that on Wednesday at 3:00 p.m., we'll meet in the construction trailer. Be prepared to give me a brief progress report on what has been completed and what's remaining to be done. We'll then walk the homes. It would be good to have ABC's field boss meet us at lot #1 at 3:15 p.m. to walk the homes with us. That way we can fine tune the priorities together and have two days to get them completed.

At 4:00 p.m. on Friday we'll meet here again and you can give me a final progress report. We can then walk the homes together. Be prepared to let me know if you had it to do over what you would do the same and what you would do differently. Mike, I'm counting on you to give it your best, make good decisions keeping the goal in mind. Clear enough?"

Let's summarize the scenario. Did you recognize where Mike's supervisor followed the **Six Steps of effective delegation** as again outlined here?

1. **Establish the Goal**
2. **Set Expectations**
3. **Set Deadlines**
4. **Set Reference Points**
5. **Provide Support**
6. **Debrief & Evaluate**

Of course, this could have been handled several different ways. But, as long as the best spirit of the main steps to effective delegation are used you can expect immediate and long term results.

How do you think Mike would feel and what type of growth potential and morale would have been accomplished if he had been told, *"You will get those ten homes ready by Friday, no excuses, or it's your butt...and don't bother me about it, I got my own problems. Just get it done!"* Sound severe? You would be surprised how common that type of "delegation" goes on in offices, factories, and business situations. That type of leader rarely advances very far and limits their success significantly. Worse yet, they hamper the progress of others.

Delegation is a <u>two way street</u>. Just because you can do something doesn't necessarily mean you should. Imbed this rule in your mind:

> **NEVER DO SOMETHING THAT SOMEONE ELSE CAN DO AS WELL OR THAT YOU CAN COACH THEM TO DO AS WELL**

<u>A major role of leaders is to always be bringing others along.</u> That means giving others a chance - even when you know they won't start out doing it as well as you. Your goal as a leader should be to **GROW** people to be able to assume larger roles. One of the best ways to accomplish this is

through **effective delegation.**

Jack Welch, former CEO of General Electric, was instrumental in leading his company, especially during the 1990s, to be acknowledged as one of the best and most profitable on the planet. He's quoted as saying:

"I think any company that's trying to play in the 1990s has got to find a way to engage the mind of every single employee. If you're not thinking all the time about making every person more valuable, you don't have a chance. What's the alternative? Wasted minds? Uninvolved people? A labor force that's angry or bored? That doesn't make sense!"

His advice is as relevant in the 2000s as then. In fact, good leadership is timeless. Good leadership a thousand years ago and a thousand years from now will still remain the same. It does not change with the seasons, styles or the times.

CONCLUSION

You now have insights into **How to Delegate** effectively, the benefits of it and the criteria for how to identify **Achievers** who are your core subjects.

Once **Achievers** are identified and you have **delegated** greater responsibilities to them and they have responded and grown as a result, you have <u>succeeded</u> in a major category of leadership.

Knowing the correct way to **effectively delegate** is

essential to accomplishing your role as a good leader. As stated earlier, **delegation** is a <u>two-way street</u>. You give and you get and it benefits the giver, the getter and the organization.

 *Grow people!*

5

UNDERSTAND THE *"POWER"* OF *EMPOWERMENT*

LEVERAGE IS THE KEY

Empowerment is a powerful leadership tool. Like any tool one must learn to use it skillfully. Good leaders become so because they have learned how to gain the greatest leverage from it. This chapter is devoted to defining its facets, applications and benefits.

It is an oversimplification to define *Empowerment* as giving a person unlimited power to carry out a task, goal or mission within a given framework. It encompasses so much more.

Empowerment is a term that incorporates a philosophy, a concept, a mechanism, a method and, some say, even a technology. It is simple in its complexity. Yet, trying to define it in a few sentences or even a paragraph, may not do it justice.

Empowerment includes giving employees greater authority that <u>requires them to begin exercising leadership skills</u>. It is the next level up from delegation and, like delegation, is a two-way street in which leaders now have a responsibility for <u>creating the environment</u> for it to work.

GETTING STARTED

The first step in that process is to *Empower* **yourself** by thinking like an owner - <u>about your job, your life, your company</u>. Owners have a proprietary sense. they focus on results, regardless of who's watching.

The next step is to understand what everyone is seeking:

Companies

- Strategic advantage
- Increased profits
- ROI for shareholders

Leaders

- Solutions to their responsibilities of achieving greater results with fewer resources *("Doing more with less!")*

Employees

- Opportunity
- Job security
- Ownership
- Recognition and a sense of pride in their work

Empowerment is a cutting edge leadership "technology" that works through people by addressing the **strategic advantage companies are seeking, the answers that leaders are seeking and the opportunities people are seeking.**

The success of these "prizes" revolves around **good leadership**; especially those leaders who are good teachers. That doesn't mean they have to be Harvard "B" school professors. As Kahlil Gibran writes in his book, *The Prophet*, *"Good teachers reveal that which already lies half asleep in the dawning of our knowledge."*

THE ESSENCE OF EMPOWERMENT

We are in an era of fierce global competition. In order to meet this challenge successfully we must produce at a lower cost with better quality and at a faster pace than our competitors. In the process we must be relentless in growth and meeting our goals. The only way to do this effectively is through people.

Leaders feel the stress of producing more with fewer people and with a wider span of responsibilities. It's for those reasons that the traditional management model of "the manager in control and the employees being controlled" may not continue to work. Ken Blanchard expressed that in his book, *The 3 Keys to Empowerment*. He also said:

"In hierarchical organizations using more traditional 'command and control' management practices, the organization's human resource capacity is only partially tapped, perhaps 25 to

30 percent of capacity."

Companies that exceed that percentage have leaders who attribute a large part of their success to *Empowering* their employees. They make every employee feel as though they make a difference. That includes the janitorial staff, mail room personnel, receptionists - *everyone*. There's no room for exclusivity if you want to harness the full potential power of the people in a company.

The real essence of *Empowerment* comes from releasing the knowledge, experience and motivational power that is already in people, but is being severely underutilized.

Every person must feel that they are playing a crucial role in the success of the organization. *Empowerment* has become one of the best management mechanisms to accomplish that goal.

ROLE MODELS

One of the best methods for understanding and applying *Empowerment* is to use, as role models, those who have defined it, exercised it and succeeded by it. My father used to say, *"If you want to be good at something, hang around with those who are good at it and do like they do."*

So, let's hang around with a few of those type people. To start with we'll go back a few years to 1979 when Chrysler Corporation was in deep financial difficulty and was on the verge of going out of business. High profile auto executive, Lee Iacocca, was brought in as a leader to pull them out of the problems created by years of poor leadership. Iacocca's reputation was the ability to marshal resources and create an environment of ***Empowerment*** to motivate others in order to get the job done.

Do you believe that any one individual, single handedly, without help, can succeed at a task as daunting as that? Don't bet on it! Do you think he knew how to delegate and ***Empower*** effectively? You can bet on it! But then, let him answer that. In his 1988 book titled, *Talking Straight*, he gave us an insight into a major premise for his success with this quote:

> *"I think a big part of my job is what I call*
> *'defining the envelope,' or setting the limits*
> *within which line management can operate*
> *on a relatively free wheeling basis."*

He was a proponent of ***Empowerment*** long before it became the popular management philosophy it is today. He exercised the concept by being a great evaluator of people. As your performance progressed, so did the challenging tasks that he dispensed until the point where he could ***define the envelope*** within which to allow *relative freewheeling*.

Setting the ***envelope*** is a lot like the game of tennis. There are boundaries and a net. As long as you keep the ball within boundaries and out of the net you can *"freewheel"* the way you play. You can hit the ball six inches above the net or six feet. It doesn't matter. But, you must keep it within the ***envelope***. Those players with the best developed skills within that ***envelope*** will win more matches, gain greater recognition and rewards.

There are some coaches who advocate only one way of doing something. They tend to stifle a person's development. Then there are those innovators who allow each player to develop their own best strengths by trying newer and better ways. *Empowerment* is a lot like that. So is good leadership.

However, there are still many leaders who fear that approach. I can hear them now, *"Oh, heavens, that's insane. It's a surefire method of getting burned!"* They then go back to being micromanagers struggling to meet objectives. Their fear is that *Empowering* people, even though they have proven performance records, means abdicating their responsibilities. **Is that really the case?**

Looking at how a very successful leader would answer that question you'll need some background on him. On the soft cover version of a former national best seller, *NUTS!*, there is a picture of a man with a rolled up sleeve exposing a tattoo that reads, *"STILL NUTS...AFTER ALL THESE YEARS."* That man is the CEO of Southwest Airlines (SWA), Herb Kelleher. He is, by far, one of the best examples, if not the best example I've ever come across of success through *Empowerment of people*.

The book, *NUTS!*, is the story of how SWA came into being during deregulation of the airline industry in the 1970s. It has since become one of our country's most successful airlines. That, in and of itself, puts him in the minority for that industry is one of the most difficult to operate in profitably. It's just possible that he knows something about leadership and especially *Empowerment*. Here's how he confronts the argument about getting burned:

"The costs of getting burned once in a while are insignificant compared to the benefits that come from people feeling free to take risks and be creative."

Herb Kelleher has created an environment which supports and encourages employees to take well defined risks without fear of retribution if they fail. This concept challenges many of the basic organizational structures that have become all to commonplace.

Individuals, and especially teams, are more receptive to leadership approaches that bring them closer to the core of what they value. That leads to better performance. **Those organizations that adopt and adapt that approach have a greater chance for success.**

Jack Welch, during his 25 year tenure as CEO of General Electric, guided GE to become one of the most profitable and well run companies on the planet. He did this through a concept he coined as *"boundarylessness."* This was a core value used to change a corporate culture from one of being bureaucracy driven to a culture of *Empowerment*.

BUILDING A CULTURE OF EMPOWERMENT

To get the most leverage and success from *Empowerment*, an entirely new environment must be created that focuses on changing attitudes, behaviors and practices about being willing to take risks. However, don't expect it to be embraced right off the bat. Why? Here are just four reasons why everyone won't "buy-in" at first. They are presented as thought provoking questions:

1. *Who wants to answer for situations that go sour because they were not given the support and authority to go along with the responsibility?*

2. *Who wants to take on a responsibility for which they were never given adequate training, information, power or rewards?*

3. *Is everyone who is capable prepared to take on such challenges?*

4. *Can people operate effectively in a newly established culture without first dismantling old attitudes and practices?*

There is a basic axiom in leadership, **"People will support what they help to create."** Therefore, you must create an environment that overcomes those fears and objections, by including your employees in on the process of establishing a culture of *Empowerment.* Start by implementing the **ODS THREE STEP** system:

1. ORGANIZE

- Flatten out your organization chart. Set-up a hub and spoke system. You are the hub at the center and the spokes are the connections between you and your team members. That's an *Empowered* organization.

2. DEPUTIZE

- *Empower* your people by giving them autonomy to carry out their jobs within a certain defined framework. In other words: set boundaries and allow them **"boudarylessness"** within.

- **Encourage** independent thinking.

- **State** a clear mission.

- **Provide** the tools, facilities, atmosphere.

3. SUPERVISE

- **Continually provide them** with the training and guidance that will help them be successful in their jobs.

- **Be a resource,** mentor, coach, counselor, teacher, rather than a boss with a controlling approach.

- **Encourage** people, giving them guidance necessary to work within boundaries.

- **Support** them when they take risks. Counsel them if they fail. Compliment them for trying and remove any fear of retribution for failure.

- **Use** risk taking failures as an opportunity to develop loyalty by showing you still support them and expect them to continue toward future successes. Colloquially put, *"If you ain't makin' mistakes, you ain't gettin' better!"*

- <u>**Celebrate**</u> their successes.

- <u>**Share information**</u> and keep them informed continually to avoid the rumor mill.

- **Get out of the way** <u>and let them do their jobs</u>.

THE BENEFITS OF <u>ODS</u>

When people see that their contributions are valued, their dignity and self respect are <u>enhanced</u>. They feel that their work, ideas and decisions can make a difference and that the success of their organization is directly related to their own success. Your <u>success</u> as an organization will come from *Empowering* your employees.

Why is that?

Because it **promotes** an attitude of:

- *"I'm respected for what I do!"*

- *"My job is important!"*

- *"My teammates need me!"*

This **leads** to:

- **Increased productivity**

- **Reduced**
  - **Absenteeism**
  - **Tardiness**
  - **Turnover**
- **Higher Morale**

All of this ultimately leads to progress, growth and increased profitability.

(Stop here and begin to think of some ways to immediately kick-off a culture of Empowerment in your organization. Then read on and see how close you came to some of the suggested ways.)

SUGGESTED WAYS TO KICK-OFF A CULTURE OF *EMPOWERMENT*
---

1. **Put up a scoreboard** that shows information on a weekly, monthly or quarterly basis such as:
   - **Stock** price
   - **Sales to date** compared to business plan
   - **Deadlines** for projects and % complete

2. **Share detailed information** with staff that brings them up to date on how the company is doing in reference to announced plans.

3. **Share your plan** for establishing a culture of *Empowerment* as follows:
   - **Acknowledge** that you know there may be some reticence based on reasons out-

lined earlier on why employees may not embrace the program immediately. Ask for everyone's patience and support.

- **Sell them** on the benefits for them.

- **Comfort them** that this won't be a meat clever approach to change. It will begin gradually.

- **As a pilot program** begin choosing someone or a team to start with. Follow-up by gradually establishing an environment from what you've learned here for building a culture of *Empowerment*. Let that person, or team, be an example for others to see. Let them become your best salespeople. Then, include everyone.

- **Be patient!** Stick with the program until you begin to see it catch hold. If there are set-backs, weather them. By so doing you'll impress upon your staff that you are serious. That will motivate them to help make it work.

You may come up with some even better ideas. If so, use them. Remember: *Empower* **yourself first.**

 *Step aside!*

6

"E R R" YOUR WAY TO NEGOTIATING EXCELLENCE

THE *"DOLPHIN"* APPROACH IS BEST

*N*egotiating is the ultimate challenge for any business person. Being good at it is essential for success. you don't have to be a shark to succeed. The *"dolphin"* approach is always better. The difference is one of style. While sharks try to intimidate people, causing fear and mistrust, dolphins genuinely enjoy people. They are confident, energetic and assertive in a most positive way.

Here are **Three Key** dolphin principles to *E R R* your way to becoming a better negotiator almost immediately:

KEY 1. *E*XERCISE SELF-DISCIPLINE

Self-discipline can be defined as, *"Do what you must do, when you must do it, whether you feel like it or not."* Yes, it requires the effort to prepare (anything worthwhile requires effort). There is an axiom in negotiating, *"The best prepared party gets the biggest piece of the pie."* Dig for the facts. Do your homework. Find out all you can about the other party such as: their goals, needs, interests and problems.

Your awareness of these things helps you to create acceptable solutions. The term, *"Win-Win"* situation may be overused, but it is most relevant to a successful outcome. This will help make others more receptive to your ideas and gives you the advantage.

An excellent method for this is found in the chapter titled, *The 66-Question Customer Profile*, in the book, *How to Swim With The Sharks Without Being Eaten Alive*, by Harvey MacKay (New York, William Morrow Company, Inc.).

A disciplined negotiator never becomes emotionally involved with the situation. (The cigar chomping "table pounder" getting his way is Hollywood, not the real world.)

Remain emotionally detached. **Be agreeably disagreeable.** In other words, don't disagree, agree and change: *"I see your point. However, have you considered_____?"* Arguing creates defensiveness. That works against you. So, do what will work for you.

KEY 2. REINFORCE CONTINUALLY

Reinforcement builds the type of confidence you want in the other party. The way to guide a person toward this confidence is to let them reinforce what you are saying. In negotiating it seems to be the human condition that what you say will be suspect, whereas what they say is gospel truth. Therefore, get them to say it by ending your statement with a question that requires positive reinforcement, such as:

- *"That's clear, isn't it?"*
- *"You understand that, don't you?"*
- *"You can see the value in that, can't you?"*
- *"That makes sense, doesn't it?"*

Ask the questions in a calm, conversational manner, but authoritatively.

KEY 3. REHEARSE, REHEARSE, REHEARSE

- **Anticipate** and prepare for as many predictable responses, obstacles and objections as possible.

- **Prepare** your responses in advance.

- **Role play** with someone knowledgeable about the situation.

The statement attributed to Thomas Edison said it best: ***"Genius is 10% inspiration and 90% perspiration."***

Preparation and rehearsal is the perspiration of negotiating genius. The American astronauts found few surprises on the moon and functioned very effectively because of their disciplined rehearsals under simulated conditions here on earth.

If you want to become a better negotiator, follow through on this exercise: **Take a 3x5 card and write vertically on it in large letters, E R R.** Then, write next to them what they mean. Allow some space between the letters for a few short notes. This will now fit in the palm of your hand and may well be the shortest, yet most effective negotiating manual ever. Here's an example:

Exercise self discipline
Find out all you can about the other party: goals, interests, problems.

Reinforce continually
"That's clear, isn't it?"
"That makes sense, doesn't it?"

Rehearse, rehearse
Anticipate objections.
Prepare responses.
Role play.

Review it frequently. Remember the guidelines for each **Key**, as outlined above, until it becomes second nature. By applying these principles with fair and ethical behavior, you'll **gain the edge**, no matter how slight. That will build on your leadership skills and help you gain the type of recognition that puts you ahead of the pack.

CONCLUSION

Aristotle gave us good advice when he said, *"We are what we repeatedly do. Excellence, then, is not an act, but a habit."*

Now that you know this, go forth and *"E R R"* your way to negotiating excellence and greater leadership recognition.

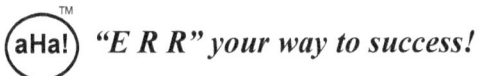 *"E R R" your way to success!*

7

MAKING *TIME* FOR *TIME MANAGEMENT*

"Persistent people begin their success where others end in failure."
- Edward Eggleston

MAKING TIME FOR WHAT YOU DON'T HAVE TIME TO DO

*W*e get so wrapped up in doing *"stuff"* every day that we let our **Time** and **Talents** erode and fail to accomplish worthwhile goals because we feel inundated with time constraints. If we only had that elusive *"one more hour."*

Time management requires setting long-range goals and then preparing near term plans to accomplish those goals. Keep in mind that a long-range goal requires the accomplishment of a series of near term connected goals. As a result, near term time management is where we feel the greatest pressures and stresses.

SELF-MANAGEMENT

Self-management is ongoing and not something we do only once, occasionally or when the mood may strike us.

Your time and talents are unique personal resources, which you alone can manage. In essence, <u>this is all we have to offer</u> and can really manage. Properly harnessing and tenaciously <u>managing your time and talents</u> will lead to a solid plan for achieving your goals.

At different times of the day or week or month, you may feel "out of control." You believe that the management of your time has slipped away from you and is now in the hands of others. Once you have come to this conclusion it's hard to take back control. The key is <u>never</u> lose it. If you do, then <u>gain it back</u>. In order to be successful at leading others you must always be in control of yourself.

"I DON'T HAVE TIME TO..."

There is a mantra that far too many capable people hide behind when they can't get things done:

"I don't have time to...

        ...return all my phone calls."
        ...plan my day."
        ...organize my files."

There is an initial step you can take to begin dealing with those issues. Start by making a list of the activities, which you *"Don't have time to do."*

1. _____

2. _____

3. _____

4. _____

5. _____

Now, read the list to yourself and this time substitute the phrase, *"I don't really want to...return all my phone calls."* Once you have completed this exercise, consider your feelings as you read the list again:

- **Are there any you agreed with?**
- **Are there any you disagreed with?**
- **Did you learn anything about yourself?**

Those things you say you don't have time to do and you really don't want to do are just excuses (choices?) you have already made *"not to do."* You will benefit by reorganizing to where they are not necessary or consolidating them to reduce the number of tasks.

You will benefit by that constant restructuring because they are wasting valuable time and energy. Be careful about delegating "drudge" work to others without also giving them the same freedom of *"boundarylessness"* as suggested earlier.

By continuing to put off activities that must be done you build stress in your day. This causes you to waste time by constantly thinking about them. That saps valuable energy when you or someone else, at your direction, could be doing them! Therefore, you must recognize the major time wasters in your life and take steps to correct them.

The **three biggest** time killers are the **"3 Ps"**:

1. **Procrastination**
2. **Poor planning**
3. **Personal disorganization**

OVERCOMING PROCRASTINATION

If you're motivated, but find it hard to get started, keep in mind Woody Allen's observation, *"Eighty percent of success is just showing up!"* That can be translated to, ***"Face the situation!"***

Here are some ways to face and overcome procrastination:

- **Break a large job down into smaller parts.** (Remember the answer to the question, *"How do you eat an elephant?" "One bite at a time."*)

- **Do the easy parts first.**

- **Face unpleasant tasks squarely.**

- **Set allotted times to deal with situations.**

- **Treat yourself after with a suitable reward.**

The next 20 percent involves planning and being personally organized. When you have a plan and things are orderly and at your fingertips the rest flows more smoothly. That's better than looking at a mess and wondering where anything is and how to get started.

Personal Time Wasters
(The enemy of good planning)

Review the list of 34 items and circle the <u>six</u> items that are your biggest time wasters. As you review the items you've circled consider each carefully. Is it a time waster? Many of us sometimes view time wasters as activities that are intrinsic to our jobs. For example, if you spend two hours a day on the telephone to service your customers, the telephone is not a time waster. Whereas, if personal and social conversations are taking up one of the two hours, you are wasting time. *(If you circled more than six you may have a bigger problem than you think.)*

1. **Incomplete information and data for solutions to problems**

2. **Attempting too much**

3. **Peer demands**

4. **Unrealistic time estimates**

5. **Lack of delegation**

6. **Putting things off for later that need done now**

7. **Telephone**

8. **Lack of organization**

9. **Equipment failure**

10. **Failure to listen**

11. **Waiting for answers**

12. Doing it yourself

13. Interruptions

14. Unable to say "No"

15. Meetings without agendas

16. Indecision

17. Lack of priorities

18. Delegating responsibility without authority

19. Crisis management

20. Involving unnecessary people

21. Conflicting priorities

22. Bypassing the chain of command

23. Outside unrelated activities

24. Snap decisions

25. Poor communication

26. Blaming others

27. Mistakes of others

28. Personal activities

29. Inadequate follow-up

30. Cluttered work area

31. Inadequate filing system

32. Over involvement with details

33. Red tape

34. Socializing

| TIME WASTER ACTION PLAN |

Now that you have taken that most important first step toward identifying ways in which you waste time you can move positively to correct them. Here's an exercise to help you get rid of your time wasters. List the time waster and then develop an **ACTION PLAN** to correct it. Here's a suggested format to help you get started:

1. My time waster is _____   _____

2. This time waster is caused by _____

3. If I keep this up, what will happen? _____

_____

4. My personal pay-off for doing something about this time waster will be _____

5. I will know I am making progress when _____

_____

6. My plan of action on this time waster is to _____

_____

(Make copies of this format and do the same with other time wasters you identified. If you're really serious about managing your time better then put the completed

ACTION PLANS in a folder. Review them daily until they become ingrained and you have taken steps to correct them.)

Special attention must be made to one of the biggest and most common enemies of time management:

INTERRUPTIONS

Often the "interrupter" gets their problem solved and then you have to go back to yours and are now even <u>further</u> <u>behind</u> the time constraint curve. It's a two-way street. Therefore, respect others. As often as possible, *"Neither an 'interrupter' nor 'interruptee' be."* Here's how to accomplish that:

- **Set limits.**

- **Get to the point.**

- **Deal with the issue on the spot** (and only that issue rather than become "tangential" and be led down the path of, *"While we are at it, another issue is..."*).

- **Conclude the conversation firmly.** Let callers leave a message. Yes, call them back and acknowledge their call. However, indicate you're working on another issue. Set-up a telephone appointment in the near future where you can devote the time necessary to address their issues.

- **If necessary, find a quiet place** outside the office for resolving or working on crucial items.

THE KEY TO PERSONAL ORGANIZATION

The key is **self-management**. There are certain basic skills that should be developed in order to achieve this effectively. The most difficult part is breaking some of the old habits and replacing them with new ones. Successfully managing activities during the time you are allotted requires that you effectively apply your skills to these four basic functions:

1. Planning

2. Organizing

3. Directing

4. Controlling

Your success is dependent on how well these four skills are developed and applied. Whether you are an executive, manager, supervisor, military leader, entrepreneur, home-maker or student you are responsible for:

PLANNING

This considers:

- **What needs to be done**
- **How it will be done**
- **Who will do what**
- **Goal setting and establishing strategies for achieving them.** *(This is covered in greater*

detail in the SETTING ATTAINABLE GOALS chapter.)

The two essentials needed for good planning are:

1. **An Annual Plan** - This allows you to see major professional and personal events such as important meetings, trips, seminars, vacations and family dates. Write these activities/events on a 12 month calendar page in order to see your year at a glance.

2. **Quarterly Goals** - This page should provide brief action statements for planned accomplishments for that given quarter. Determine the most important to the least important goals for that quarter by sequencing each goal. Pick realistic due dates to aid in the work flow.

ORGANIZING

Personal disorganization is a major time waster. A key function of time management involves organizing tasks, projects and activities to achieve your objectives while conserving your resources, energy and time. It establishes:

- **What work needs to be done**
- **Who shall do it**
- **Authority**
- **Responsibility**
- **Deadlines**

Many desks are cluttered with an appointment calendar, an address and telephone directory, message pads, scraps of paper with miscellaneous notes and suspense files. While each tool can be useful, often times the combination of these various methods contributes to disorganization. Important notes or paper shuffled between desks, pockets and briefcases are often left behind, lost or misplaced. A wise organizational rule of thumb is:

> **Organize your paper flow so that you don't have to handle a piece of paper more than once.**

Try adopting the **ARF** method of organizing paper flow. Set-up three file areas:

A - ACTION - Place everything in this file that needs either your immediate personal attention or action or is pending future action.

R - REVIEW - Place everything in this file that you expect you will need to review from time to time such as, business plans, bulletins, company guidelines, regular reference material.

F - FILE - This is the file for your copies of correspondence sent, received, items completed and historical data.

Any remaining action items that can be delegated or

sent to the person or department closest to the situation for their attention should be handled accordingly. Anything that doesn't fall into these categories or guidelines should be discarded.

It's ok to organize files within these categories. For instance, your "tickler" file (usually an accordion file numbered 1 - 31, denoting the days of the month) could be in the **ACTION** file area. You could have a separate file that is marked **"IMMEDIATE ACTION."** The rest of the items would go into the tickler file in accordance with the day of the month designated for attention. Each day you would "tickle" the file by pulling out those items filed for action on that particular day.

A very common practice is to set-up a "pending file." Be careful with that as it could become a catch-all for too many things and soon begins to bulge. If you establish a certain time frame within which an item should be handled by using the tickler file for future **ACTION** items, that becomes your pending file.

The difference is it establishes a time frame within which something should be handled. If, on the established day it's not, then follow-up. If still no response then discard because it obviously wasn't that important to begin with. Napoleon is reputed to have set aside pending problem requests for two weeks. He reasoned that within that time the problems would have resolved themselves.

Self-management experts are in agreement that improving personal productivity requires the utilization of some type of organizational system. This is necessary to coordinate the multiple demands and priorities of one's personal and professional life. Whether you use a PDA, preprinted forms or make up your own forms, some type of organizational system is essential. Another wise rule of thumb is:

> **Self-management skills and personal productivity can be improved by utilizing a comprehensive system that is simple to understand and easy to use.**

As common and familiar as it is, the humble **"To Do"** list is still one of the best time management tools to use, **PROVIDED** it is used properly. Many individuals don't really use this tool effectively. Writing a bunch of items on a list doesn't necessarily make you a good time manager. Here's a way to get the most out of your list:

- **Compile** the *To Do* list at the end of the work day for the next day.

- **Keep** the list to no more than six items being realistic about what can be accomplished.

- **Set** priorities starting with the most important item first, not necessarily the most urgent - there is a difference. Often these "urgent" items overshadow the more important ones. You must be astute enough to differentiate between them. If they are one in the same, fine. However, you may find that more often they are not. There is an old analogy that focusing on the "urgent" at the expense of the important is like straightening up the deck chairs on the Titanic as it's heading toward the iceberg.

- **Sequence** each of the items on your list and establish time estimates for each.

- **Most importantly**, everything that must be done tomorrow should be set-up and scheduled before you leave work.

DIRECTING

This involves:

- **Delegating**

- **Requesting** assistance

- **Instructing,** explaining and issuing orders and describing the specifics of a job

- **Indicating** the what and how of assignments in a manner conducive to cooperation and excellence

CONTROLLING

This function pertains to:

- **All of the activities** for which you are responsible

- **The proper use** and integration of resources and activities

- **Insuring** performance of the right kind, at the right time, at the right place

- **Avoiding** waste, conflict and duplication

Once your plan is underway you must take responsibility for staying on course, remaining focused on your priorities, monitoring and following-up on all activities. Valuable tools for carrying out the four time management functions outlined here are:

- **Monthly calendars**

- **Daily schedules**

- **Delegation**

- **Communication records**

- **Planning schedules**

SUMMARY

This 17 point summary covers the salient points of what has been outlined above plus some additional ways to help you make better use of your time:

1. **Develop** a systematic approach for managing your time by utilizing these three time saving techniques:

   - **Write it down immediately**

- Use abbreviations
- Set-up a visual reminder system

2. **Focus** on projects that you are convinced will provide you with the greatest long-term benefits.

3. **Set** self-imposed deadlines.

4. **Make** a *"To Do"* list daily.

5. **Set priorities** for tasks and projects. Use this format for prioritizing:

   - **Rank tasks** in order of importance
   - **Build in time** for the unexpected
   - **Leave time** for thinking and planning
   - **Remain flexible**
   - **Realize** you won't finish everything

6. **Schedule activities** on a master calendar: monthly, weekly and daily. Use it as a "tickler" system. *(A typical tickler system is an accordion folder with 31 separations for each day of the month. Place action items in the specific date slot of the folder when it needs action. "Tickle" the folder every day by reviewing the action items necessary for the current date and review the other dates to remain alert to what is coming up.)*

7. **Concentrate your efforts** on only one thing at a time rather than jumping around and ending up

with a lot of half completed unrelated items.

8. **Delegate** everything you can to others.

9. **Eliminate** unnecessary tasks.

10. **Plan time** for interruptions.

11. **Set-up** availability hours and "quiet time."

12. **Learn** to say *"No"* constructively.

13. **Try not** to work on weekends (unless you're a minister).

14. **Give** yourself time off as a special reward when you've accomplished important tasks.

15. **Don't** waste time regretting failures or feeling guilty about what you didn't get done.

16. **Remind** yourself, *"There is always enough time for the important things."*

17. **Do it now!**

CONCLUSION

You now have some common sense concepts to help you manage your time better. As a result of adopting and adapting them you'll become a more effective leader in the process.

If you set your goals, establish your priorities, then **plan**, **organize**, **direct** and **control** your activities, your life becomes <u>fuller, richer, more rewarding and less stressful</u>. In addition you sure will get one *heck'uv* a lot more accomplished!

 **Duh! Write it down!**

8

CONFLICT RESOLUTION

WHAT EVERY LEADER MUST KNOW

*M*uch has been written about this topic mainly focusing on what to do as opposed to *how* to do it. The human condition sometimes requires a cool objective party to arbitrate differences of opinions. Usually, that person is the leader of the group - the party with the final word. Therefore, your immediate approach to situations and subsequent actions determines the outcome.

Typically, in most conflict resolutions, there is a satisfied party and one not so satisfied. The ideal method is to end the conflict with everyone coming out whole and <u>satisfied that it was fairly handled</u> (even though they may not have gotten all they wanted). A good leader tries to accomplish this by seeing all sides of an issue and then proceeds to resolve it accordingly.

Conflicts come in many sizes, degrees and intensities.

Whether you call them problems, issues, differences, disagreements or confrontations, they all come under the heading of *conflict*. There seems to be a certain inevitability about them. Historically speaking, they seem to pervade the human condition in a far greater consistency than we would prefer. That being the case, as good leaders, we must be students of the human condition and develop the ability to deal with conflict.

Some conflicts are explosive whereas others seethe beneath the surface. They then erupt at the most inopportune times. In most cases they <u>could have been prevented</u> if addressed properly early on. The latter are the type that good leaders should recognize and proactively attempt to defuse before they emulate Mount St. Helens.

There is a **FIVE STEP** process that is most helpful in accomplishing that necessary goal:

1. MAKE THE BEST OF IT

In conflict we deal with values, beliefs and expectations. This can differ from person to person. It's a fact of life that we are bound to have differences of opinion. Therefore, we must make the best of every situation that comes up where differences need arbitrated. As a leader, like it or not, this is where you will spend a lot of time and energy.

The upside is that <u>conflict can increase loyalty</u>. It is estimated that the majority of employees will remain loyal if they feel you have responded to their problem. They will overlook a lot. However, don't expect that they will overlook:

- **Poor time management leading to delaying or prolonging decisions**
- **Poor communications management**
- **Lying or stretching points to gloss over a situation**

How do you make the best of it and avoid the above "no-no" list? Face and resolve conflict situations **IMMEDIATELY, with fairness, honesty and integrity.** This may lead to unpopularity in some quarters, but if handled as advised here you will maintain respect.

2. ESTABLISH GROUND RULES

The secret to successful conflict resolution is to set and follow practical ground rules. In essence **SET EXPECTATIONS.** You must set boundaries within which to operate and stick with them. That's a tall order. It's easier said than done in the midst of some over-the-top confrontations you'll be faced with. The easier ones seem to get handled between the parties. But, you will always get drawn into the more difficult ones.

How do you apply the ground rules?

Encourage communication and expression <u>without allowing destructive words and behaviors</u>. Stick with it. Stop the dialog if it gets out of hand and strays from the point and proper decorum. Remind the person or parties of the ground rules and don't proceed until you get agreement.

3. LEARN TO LISTEN

There is a wise saying, *"First seek to understand, then to be understood."* In order to accomplish this listen carefully, without the intent of responding. Listen with the intent of hearing to make sure you understand the other person's perspective. Restate to them what you've heard. That is one of the most effective listening skills you can ever develop.

Here is how to listen effectively

L - Lean forward and look the speaker in the eye. Tune out or mentally mute as many external distractions as possible. Drain your mind of all other thoughts and focus as intently as possible on the speaker.

I - Use "I" statements during feedback (*"I think you could"...rather than "You need to...!"*).

S - Stay focused. What you listen for is what you hear. As stated earlier, always listen with the intent of hearing rather than with the intent to respond. That's important. When you tune out the speaker and concentrate on preparing a response you stand to miss important things they will say that may have already answered your response. Then, when you do respond and they've already answered your retort it becomes obvious you were not attentive. That will strain the situation far worse because you've demonstrated your unwillingness to listen.

T - Take notes. Make them brief. Confine them to critical information such as names, dates, places and specific numbers.

E - Eye contact. But, how can you have eye contact while you're on the telephone? Believe it or not, there is a method and it works. Here's how: Stand up. Raise your line of sight by picking an imaginary spot on the wall a few inches higher than you normally look. This helps to keep you focused because it does not allow your chin to settle into your chest which blocks your airway slightly thereby reducing oxygen intake. That could interfere with concentration and voice projection. The other party can *hear* the results of that.

This is especially obvious to a listener at the other end when you ask a question or begin a response. You come across as disinterested by your tone of voice. Try this exercise:

While seated let your chin fall and almost touch your chest. Then say, "I love you."
Now stand up. Look at an imaginary spot on the wall a few inches above your normal line of sight and say the same thing. Which of the

two responses was more convincing? Which of the two would you most like to hear or express? I believe you get the point now.

N - Nod your head. Do this in a positive way when you see the point. However, avoid nodding your head in a negative way when you disagree. It's best to keep the other party guessing on that part. Just stay still and look them in the eye. If you feel you must make some response, try just saying, "That's very interesting." That shows you are listening but are noncommittal. Staying noncommittal throughout the listening process works in your favor because it shows an objective approach. That will foster respect and go a long way toward getting cooperation.

4. KNOW YOUR OPPOSITION

You must be able to determine <u>fairly quickly</u> the maturity level and personality of the person(s) you're dealing with. That's why good leaders are perpetual students of human nature. Work on the ability to "size-up" people quickly and accurately to determine their true motives.

There are two categories of people that you will most often deal with in conflict resolution:

1. UPSET

2. DIFFICULT

Upset people are different than *difficult* people in that they provide challenge and opportunity. *Upset* people perform a service for you because they <u>identify</u> areas where you can concentrate that helps you to improve:

- **Unfair situations**
- **Poor working conditions**
- **Convoluted procedures**
- **Obsolete standards**
- **Imbalanced workloads**

In that type of adversity there is often opportunity that leads to progress, respect and loyalty.

On the other hand *difficult* people are often unreasonable <u>no matter what you do</u>. Therefore, spend <u>minimal</u> time on their situations. They are the type who will have you jumping through hoops and, no matter what you do for them, will never be satisfied.

Difficult people have a psychological need to get attention through disruptive means. That's why they are chronically hard to communicate with and to satisfy.

Good leaders know that they must deal with both types, but with emphasis on *upset*. They provide the opportunities to be turned into loyal employees, if handled properly. These type people tend to be reasonable. When a reasonable person gets *upset* they have a momentary lapse into unreasonableness, but are still <u>basically rationale</u>.

There is no single technique that works with every *upset*

person. However, there are skills that can be learned that generally work well with the majority. Always start by taking control of the situation. How? Through a **THREE STEP** process:

Step 1. Defuse the Situation
Acknowledge their anger by saying, *"I understand you're very angry right now. How can I be of help?"* By so doing you're not agreeing to give them everything they want, only to *listen.*

Step 2. Listen
This reduces the level of anger because it satisfies the first desire of an angry person: **recognition of their feelings and a sympathetic ear.** Apply the *"two minute rule"* which is to listen for the first two minutes before saying anything. A rule of thumb of when to respond is when the person starts to repeat themselves.

Step 3. Begin the Dialog
You have taken control by *DEFUSING* the situation, guiding the *upset* party to begin talking by showing your willingness to *LISTEN.* This has a great calming effect.

Establish a rapport from the very beginning by putting all parties at ease thereby reducing the tension. Begin by establishing a ***community of agreements***. That consists of all of the items brought to your attention that you are reasonably certain all parties would accept. Once that has been accomplished (call it getting to the *"yesses"* first), it's usually much easier to get cooperation when dealing with the controversial area.

You have now positioned yourself to proceed with your side of the issue by bringing up points in a <u>non-threatening</u> way, such as, *"I regret this happened and can see how that can make you upset. However, have you considered_____?"*

5. NEGOTIATE A COMPROMISE

The goal in any disagreement should be to seek a <u>mutually agreeable solution</u> where everybody wins something. Granted, that may not always be possible. In any event the outcome should be fair to all parties.

An effective way to accomplish this is to discuss possible options. Then, have the individual(s) list their complaints in writing in an outline format showing only the facts rather than a long narrative. After your review, evaluate them together and find an outcome which would most likely be acceptable by all parties through a negotiated compromise.

SUMMARY

Resolving conflict revolves primarily around:

- **Fairness**
- **Honesty**
- **Taking control**

- **Setting expectations**

- **Learning to listen**

- **Sizing-up the people involved** to determine who the rational parties are and who the difficult parties are

- **Negotiating a compromise** that does not undermine personal respect, fair treatment and ethical business practices

---

 *Do the right thing, no matter what!*

9

SETTING
"ATTAINABLE"
GOALS

ARE YOUR GOALS ATTAINABLE?
*A*ll too often, with good intentions, we set goals that we hope we can achieve. You know the type. They usually begin with, *"Someday I'm going to..."* and someday never comes (be honest).

Don't lull yourself into thinking that *hope* is a plan. When we do this, it sets us up for disappointment. When you fail at achieving those type goals, you start believing that you can't achieve any goals. Therefore, you have a tendency to give up and let life and happenstance take over. The results are rarely satisfactory.

This chapter has been designed to help you set attainable goals and objectives that are important to you and achieve them. You will learn an easy no-nonsense approach to identifying your goals and objectives and the skills to make them a reality. Upon completion of this chapter you will learn why it's important to:

- **Understand why** previous goals were not achieved
- **Identify goals** that are important and *attainable*
- **Use *"MAPS"*** as a guideline to measure your goals
- **Determine** the activities necessary to achieve each goal

THE ADVENTURE OF SETTING GOALS

Many of us enjoy good adventure movies and books. They capture our attention and our imagination. At times we may even find ourselves "caught up" in the adventure.

Life should have elements of high adventure. Facing unknown challenges in our lives and our organizations has many of the same elements of exploring unknown worlds.

How does an adventure story relate to setting and achieving goals? Believe it or not, when you set a goal, it is very much like an adventure movie or book. A simple comparison can be made between the **FIVE BASIC PARTS** of adventure movies, books and setting and achieving goals.

The FIVE BASIC PARTS Comparison:

1. A main character - yourself

2. Activating event - something happens to make

you want to set a goal

3. Set of clues - you put the steps together that will allow you to achieve the goal

4. The journey - you start accomplishing the steps required to achieve the goal

5. Change - you achieve the goal and have changed

So, life can imitate art. Our lives can follow the outlines of interesting movies, books and high adventure situations.

WHO ACHIEVES GOALS?

Over the years there have been studies about people who achieve goals and those who don't. They have discovered some very interesting facts regarding these two groups.

One of the most notable studies is the *Yale Study of Goals*. It has been widely quoted for decades in books and by well known self-help motivational speakers. While the actual study itself is difficult to find for a first hand review, the most widely accepted results of the study are:

- **87% of the MBA graduates did not have goals**
- **13% did have goals**
- **10% of those who had goals did not have them in writing**
- **3% who had written goals achieved 10 times more than the 97% who did not have written goals**

You don't have to be a rocket scientist to realize that the first step in achieving a goal is ***writing it down***. That being said we will focus specifically on you as a goal setter. To do so it's important that you understand your personal relationship with goals as follows:

Goals I Achieved

At one time or another, you have achieved a goal that was important to you. The goal you achieved most likely went beyond the *"wish list"* type. It included certain specifics such as, calculations, items to do and deadlines to meet.

Most likely the reasons for your success were:

- **You thought it over carefully**
- **You mapped your strategy**
- **You set out to do what was necessary**

Let's look at two goals you have achieved. On line (a) list the goal. On line (b) write down your main reason for reaching the goal.

1. (a) _____

  (b) _____

2. (a) _____

  (b) _____

Using the above information you will probably notice that there was a pattern for success. The reasons most often cited are:

- **Wrote down the goal**
- **Were passionate about the goal**
- **Planning had to be done to accomplish the goal**
- **There was a life or death situation**
- **There was a mentor's encouragement**

If you know this, then why proceed further? Good question! The answer is that, although we may be cognizant of certain actions, we may not have organized, systematized and made them a consistent discipline in our nature.

A major difference between a good week-end athlete and an Olympic athlete is: organized, systematized, consistent disciplined training. **So, go for the gold in life!** The training and discipline starts here. It's up to you how far you carry it.

Goals I Didn't Achieve

Much to our discontent, we sometimes don't accomplish certain goals we desire to achieve. A major reason is: not making an effort to understand and go through the process to make them attainable. When that occurs it leads to discouragement and the tendency to avoid setting goals. By recognizing and facing this we can then take the necessary steps that lead to achieving goals.

In this exercise make a list of two goals that you have <u>not</u> achieved. On line (a) list the goal you didn't achieve. On line (b) write down the main reason for not reaching the goal:

1. (a) _____

   (b) _____

2. (a) _____

   (b) _____

Using the above information you will probably notice that there is a pattern for not accomplishing your goals. The reasons most often cited are:

- **Didn't write them down**
- **Didn't take the time**
- **Didn't have the background**
- **Didn't really believe in the goal**

My Important Goals

It has been said, ***"Be careful of the things you want, for you will surely get them."*** That just doesn't happen by itself. It implies the knowledge and desire and a process.

The first action to achieving your important goals is to **IDENTIFY** them. The following will assist you in identifying at least one goal in each important area of your life:

FAMILY _____

CAREER _____

EDUCATION _____

FINANCIAL _____

HEALTH _____

SPIRITUAL _____

EXERCISE _____

SELF _____

Steps to Achieving Your Goals

If you follow just **SIX STEPS** each time you desire to achieve a goal, you will find out whether you have approached them realistically. The steps to achieving your goals are simple yet very effective.

You may also find that seemingly complex goals can become simplistic and attainable. These **SIX STEPS** are outlined in the box on the following page.

SIX STEPS TO ACHIEVING GOALS

1. <u>Determine</u> goals and write them down.

2. <u>Apply</u> the *MAPS Test* to each goal.

3. <u>List</u> the activities to achieve the goals.

4. <u>Sequence</u> activities in order (first to last).

5. <u>Assign</u> due dates to each activity.

6. <u>Organize</u> each activity into a planner system.

<u>What is the *MAPS Test*?</u>

This test is the *key* to the whole system. It's important to take time to put each goal through this simple and effective test to determine if it is achievable:

- Is the goal <u>*M*</u>*easurable?*
- Is the goal <u>*A*</u>*ttainable?*
- Is the goal <u>*P*</u>*ositive?*
- Is the goal <u>*S*</u>*pecific?*

<u>Sample *MAPS Test*</u>

Here is a sample of how to apply a *MAPS Test.* The goal that will be tested is: *Obtaining a Master of Business Administration (MBA) Degree. (The sample presupposes that this applies to a working adult.)*

Is the goal <u>M</u>easurable?

Twelve courses are required in order to receive an MBA and will take three years of work at night and weekends. The goal is then broken down into increments of the courses required over the time period allotted.

Is the goal <u>A</u>ttainable?

I have the prerequisite requirements to be accepted:

- *A Bachelor's Degree*
- *Required undergraduate courses and grades*
- *Have the finances available*
- *My boss and family are supportive*

Is the goal <u>P</u>ositive?

Once I have an MBA the opportunities afforded me will be greatly increased. Also, as I pursue my MBA, much of the material learned will be applicable to my present job.

Is the goal <u>S</u>pecific?

The goal is very specific because the total focus is on obtaining an MBA. I will know I have completed the goal and achieved it when I have satisfied all of the requirements and march down the aisle to receive my degree. *(It should be noted at this point that visualizing that moment of success can be a very powerful motivator.)*

The *MAPS Test* takes only a short time of concentrated effort. It makes it very obvious what goals you can achieve. The *MAPS Test* guides you toward those goals where you have the best chances for success.

SUMMARY

As with any new skill or ability, there are always guidelines. Here is a summary of the **SIX** most important ones. They are *"must do"* items to become successful in making your goals *attainable*. Approach them on the basis of these personal affirmations:

If I want to achieve my goals:

1. *I must* determine my goals and write them down.

2. *I must* give my goals the MAPS Test.

3. *I must* list the activities to achieve my goals.

4. *I must* sequence activities in order (first to last).

5. *I must* assign due dates to each activity.

6. *I must* organize each activity into a planner system.

CONCLUSION

Setting and achieving *attainable* goals is not difficult if you put them through the steps outlined here. Approach your goals as high adventure challenges. By adopting that attitude and following the guidelines presented in this chapter you could achieve goals not otherwise attempted. That could be <u>life changing</u>.

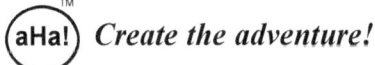 *Create the adventure!*

10

BUILDING *TRUST* IS MORE IMPORTANT THAN BEING RIGHT ALL THE TIME

WHAT SHOULD YOU EMPHASIZE?
Trust is one of the most important parts of any relationship. How much you can trust a person, be they family, a friend, fellow worker, or a love interest, determines how open and healthy your relationship will be.

If we approach the concept of *Trust* as a <u>confident expectation</u>, then we can begin to develop the premise that: *It's better to be trusted than to be right all the time.*

Why is that the case?

The higher the leadership position, where taking risks is expected, the greater the chances of making mistakes. When you must take risks the landscape usually abounds with mine fields of inevitable errors. Experienced leaders know they can't be right all of the time. They also know they must continually maintain the respect and confidence of their followers.

Why is this important?

When you build trust in others you establish the confident expectation that you will always be *honest, fair* and *ethical.* People will forgive mistakes and continue to respect, support and follow leaders who acknowledge mistakes.

Immature leaders, on the other hand, feel erroneously that they must always be right or they will lose *"face"*and the respect and confidence of their followers. You sometimes see examples of that in political leaders as well as organizations.

They feel that no one in the organization, who may have opposed or offered alternatives to a risk, should ever be made to feel they were right and their leader was wrong. This is called the *"zero defect mentality."* It creates timid leaders down the line and forces those with potential to go silent or elsewhere.

According to the *MORI* poll, conducted for the *Financial Times,* 80% of those polled believed that *"Directors of large companies cannot be trusted to tell the truth."* Two thirds of those in full-time employment say they do not believe that, *"...companies can be trusted to honor their pension commitments to employees."* Nearly 25% of workers no longer believe that company pension schemes are worth joining. Does this hint of a *"trust crisis"* in business today?

Should we be naturally distrustful of others?

Something we dislike most is to be deceived, cheated or lied to. To call someone a liar is a serious charge, often made when we are angry. It can lead to severe confrontation. Yet, common sense tells us that some distrust is appropriate.

People do deceive others, even best friends, loved ones, bosses and subordinates. This happens because, in some ways society encourages distrust. We teach children not to accept rides from strangers. We are dubious about ads and especially some television commercials. This was to the point where a *"Truth in Advertising Law"* had to be enacted. If we are so honest, then why?

We know people put their best foot forward when trying to convince us of something. Even some politicians (believe it or not) often say what they think we want to hear rather than their true agenda.

Have you ever heard a parent or manager say, in response to being advised of a telephone call, which they could take, ***"Tell them I'm not here"*** or ***"Tell them I'm in a meeting."?*** That is seemingly a small item. But, what type of message does it send to a child or staff member when they are actually told to lie? Could they interpret that as the culture of a family or organization?

Does it tell the child it's ok to eventually lie to parents? Does it do the same for a staff member and just as bad put them on alert that if you would lie about a small thing like that what would you lie to them about? *"Everybody does it,"* doesn't cut it. As Scriptures advises, ***"If you can't be trusted in small things, you can't be trusted in large things."***

Many people respond to stereotypes instead of real people. So, is it best to *trust* or *distrust?* The answer is not simple. In general, those people who put trust in others have better interpersonal relationships. <u>People low in trust tend to be more angry, competitive, resentful and unsympathetic.</u>

As individuals we are so complex and have so many feelings, needs and opinions that we can't always reveal our true selves to a new acquaintance. So, we play roles, at least we show only parts of our true selves. You've heard the old retort, *"Oh, he's not really that quiet. He loosens up when he gets to know you."*

This is a defense mechanism built over the years out of fear of rejection and our own sensitivity or vulnerability. Few people actually want to pretend to be something they aren't. They want to be accepted for who they are. However, we often tell people what we think they want to hear and what's most acceptable. If we don't then we run the risk of criticism and rejection. After all, when having a group discussion, who wants to be the first to leave?

It is most evident in the teen years where peer pressure runs rampant and defines the arena in which we must deal on a daily basis. The attitude there is to blend in with the *crowd* and be one of the *"regular guys."* The true young leaders who emerge are those who have the self-confidence to rise above the need for peer approval. They define their own path as *the right thing* to do rather than have it watered down by wondering if the *"regular guys"* would approve.

When we mature, we tend to rise above it a bit. However, there is a metamorphosis as it begins to take on a different complexion in the form of pleasing bosses, compromising to satisfy ambitions and other's expectations.

Some of this has its merits. However, should it be the defining premise upon which we build our lives? In his play *Hamlet*, Shakespeare advises us through Polonius as he counsels his son Laertes, ***"This above all: to thine own self be true..."*** That advice is applicable in <u>all</u> areas of our lives.

Why build *Trust*?

Even the best risks that were well planned and with good and just intentions can go sour. People will follow those leaders who demonstrate that they trust others, are honest, fair and ethical. This will remain even when they make mistakes <u>provided</u> that they take responsibility.

On the other hand, they will <u>not</u> always follow those leaders who are distrustful and continuously blame others for their shortcomings. Here is an axiom to remember:

> **Building *TRUST* is more <u>essential</u> to being a good leader than attempting to build the perception of being right all the time.**

The major barrier to building trust is **INSECURITY**. In fact, insecurity is a major barrier in just about all areas of good leadership development. *Insecurity* usually does not take the form of timidity. Often, quite the opposite. It is hidden or masked with an outward *"bravado"* or even *"bruskness."* An astute observer can recognize this by how arrogant, distrustful, dishonest, unfair and *"always right"* that type of person demonstrates themselves to be.

Certain types of people have a distrustful and suspicious nature which masks their insecurities. Those are difficult people to deal with because, no matter how innocent or sincere your motives, they will look for the hidden *"gotchas."* This is mainly because that's the way they would be and therefore everyone else is the same. They lack self-confidence and feel that if they admit errors no one will take them seriously again. That would lead to a rejection of them as a leader.

They will look for something, real or not, to maintain their distrustful nature. Even when shown their distrust was unfounded, they remain unforgiving. Those type people do not make good leaders because of the negative environment they create. They are the micromanagers within organizations. As a result they don't trust anyone to do an assigned task as well as they would or the same way they would. So, they continually look over everyone's shoulder stifling creativity and innovation.

How do you overcome *insecurity, fear of rejection* and *unfounded criticism?*

Among the better antidotes for insecurity and fear of rejection are self-confidence, self-acceptance and an ability to accept and profit from criticism. You cannot please everyone, nor should you even try. Those who attempt to are usually ineffectual. Down through history even the best leaders have faced unfounded criticism, accusations of dishonesty and mistrust by opponents because of biases and professional jealousy.

Abraham Lincoln, one of our most honored presidents, was often faced with that situation because of his many detractors. He followed the vital principle of:

If the criticism is correct then do something about it. If it's not, then those who matter will see it for what it is and disregard it. Those who believe it are the type of people who don't matter.

How do you handle *Criticism* and create *Trust*?

- **Avoid** over-reacting to the criticism or rejection so that you can understand what is being said about you. *(Remember, you don't have to be loved by everyone all of the time. But, make constructive use of the opinions of others.)*

- **Assess** the accuracy of what was said. Try to understand the motives of the source:
  - Are emotions being **displaced** on to you?

- Is the critic's opinion based on **valid** information?

- Are they **projecting**?

- Are they playing **"put-down"** games?

- Are they **afraid** of competing with you?

- Is there a personal **bias**?

- Is there professional **jealousy**?

- **If the criticism seems accurate** (especially if several people close to you agree), ask for all the information and help they can give. Then, take steps to improve.

- **If the criticism seems in error** and biased, then discount the information or "take it for what it's worth." It would still be valuable to understand how and why the situation arose. Depending on the circumstances, you'll have to decide whether to stand your ground and counter or forget it and move on.

The major point is that you are less vulnerable, dependent and more self-accepting and can take greater risks in trusting and relating to others. The stronger and more secure you are in yourself, the more honest you will be to others. This promotes greater openness others will have toward you.

While *trust* is an essential part of all good relationships, it is very easy to give trust before it is deserved or to give it too easily. Take this brief test:

- **Are you the type of person who trusts everybody?**

- **Do you have too much faith in other people?**

- **Can you pick-up on the signs that a person is not trustworthy?**

Clearly, distrust is appropriate in some situations. But, they are few. Applicable here is advice from the late president, Ronald Reagan, who once said, *"Trust, but verify."*

Apply the *"Trust Scale"*

Trust and *honesty* are more often preferred, especially as one becomes more secure and confident in themselves. Interesting research has confirmed the merits of trusting others. Following is a *"Trust Scale"* that measures the belief that another person's word or promise can be relied upon. To what extent do you agree with these statements?

- **In dealing with strangers,** one is better off trusting them...within reason...until they provide evidence of being untrustworthy.

- **Most people** can be counted on to do what they say they will do.

- **Most elected public officials** are really sincere in their campaign promises.

- **Most sales people** are honest in describing their products.

- **Very few accident claims** filed against insurance companies are phony.

You can get a feel for how you would answer such questions. All of these questions reflect a trusting attitude. In the extreme, though, with no "boundaries" they would reflect a naive, too trusting attitude. If you think that's to simplistic, just study 20th century history, especially WWII to see how naive and "overly" trusting certain world politicians were. It continues to this day.

Trusting, but not naive, people tend to be happier, better liked, more honest and with higher moral values than less trusting people. By the same token, not all distrustful people are dishonest themselves.

Some would say that trusting is pretty dumb. But high and low trusters are about the same in intelligence. You might think, *"OK, but surely trusters are more gullible."* Research refutes that. It's true that the high truster does take the position that, *"I'll trust them until they do me wrong."* But, they seem just as able to detect the cues of a dishonest deal or statement as a distrustful person.

Indeed, it's the distrustful person who is more likely to be *"taken"* by a con artist. Why? Since many dishonest people think they are smarter than the next person, they feel they can't be hoodwinked. That makes them easier prey for deals almost *"too good to be true."* The more trusting, moralistic person would most likely say, *"I'd rather not get involved in something borderline, dishonest or illegal."*

Another disadvantage of a distrustful nature is that it impedes honest dealings and puts up barriers, especially to open, intimate relationships. People tend to be more distrustful in competitive rather than cooperative situations. A betrayal of trust is hard for most people to forgive. But, trusting type people are more likely to give someone a *"second chance"* if they demonstrate worthiness.

How can you become more *Trusting?*

When someone says something you tend to doubt (without any hard evidence), act as though you accept it and see how they perform. If they measure up, then you will learn to be more trusting. They will be motivated to become (or remain) more trustworthy. The axiom to remember is:

> **Listen to what people say, but <u>always</u> go by what they do.**

Trust in *Consultation* and *Communication*

Trust in *Consultation* and *Communication* is essential. Studies reveal that amidst environments of high levels of uncertainty, powerful and decisive chief executives and top management teams produce better performance. Critical to their success is consultation among members of the top team and open flow of information both down the chain of command as well as back up.

Researchers have found, however, that when disaster strikes, organizations tend to restrict rather than open the flow of communication and information. Trust appears to decrease. Managers, unfortunately, tend to reduce the number of information channels they use. They are more inclined to seek supportive rather than challenging information. The best approach is:

> **Open the information taps, come clean and move on.**

Integrity and *Trust* - Evaluate Yourself

Integrity and *Trust* are the threads that connect all aspects of successful lives and businesses. Review these broad areas of leadership strata that focus on *Integrity* and *Trust* and evaluate yourself as to which you can adopt, adapt and improve upon:

Individual *Integrity* and *Trust*

- Seen as truthful
- Seen as keeping confidences and admitting mistakes
- Seen as responsible and dependable

Managerial *Courage*

- Willing to identify issues that may affect the team
- Acts to address these issues quickly
- Does not hesitate to provide useful feedback to move the group forward

Perseverance
- Pursues everything with energy and drive
- Does not give up in the face of resistance or set-backs
- Willing to invest themselves in the work at hand
- Takes pride in their work
- Maintains commitment to the task, even when difficult

Strategic Agility
- Sees ahead clearly and can anticipate and plan for reactions from others accurately
- Has a broad perspective and is future oriented
- Can see possibilities and create new ideas, strategies and plans

Time Management
- Uses their time effectively and efficiently
- Manages personal and team time well
- Expedites the flow of work
- Conducts effective meetings
- Concentrates their efforts on the important priorities, gets things done on time and works efficiently
- Can manage multiple priorities well

Dealing with Ambiguity
- Can effectively cope with change
- Can shift priorities comfortably
- Can make decisions without having the total pic-

ture
- Handles ambiguous situations well
- Considers alternatives and challenges the status quo

Interpersonal *Savvy*
- Develops effective and productive relationships with others
- Builds a network of support within the team and in the broader organization
- Relates well to all types of people
- Can manage conflicts and tense situations comfortably

Listening
- Listens attentively to others
- Attempts to understand other viewpoints
- Has the patience to hear others out, even if there is disagreement
- Is effective in both one on one and group interactions
- Understands the importance of feedback (both giving and receiving)

SUMMARY

Now that you have completed and absorbed the key points of this chapter, think of the many ways in which you can develop an attitude of trust and confidence in areas that may seem like small things. Here are a few seemingly small areas where **TRUST** begins by...

- ...**being on time** for meetings which sends a signal that you respect everyone else's time and their responsibilities.

- ...**answering** telephone messages, even if it's just to acknowledge the call and advise you're unable to divert from your current project for the moment.

- ...**asking** a staff member when they can take time to meet with you. *(It sends a signal that you respect their work.)*

- ...**respecting** an employee's personal time and not disturbing them while they are enjoying a much needed break or lunch hour. *(Believe it or not, there are some managers who revel in interrupting their people during those times just to show their power. Avoid being one of them.)*

- ...**never** *"overselling"* but, always under promising and over delivering.

- ...**always** doing the right thing, even if it impacts you negatively.

- ...**admitting** mistakes openly.

You can see the pattern here and could probably add a few more of your own. This has now become your *value statement*. It should be added to your statement of the type of leader you wish to be.

Additionally, adopt the theory of business and life: ***"Expect the best and you're likely to get it."*** It's the basis of how to treat employees, customers and others. Expect them to be honest, hard-working and trustworthy. You can be assured your trust will be rewarded.

 ***Better TRUSTED than busted!***

Summary of the (aHa!)™ Principles

(aHa!)™ *Face-to-Face!*

(aHa!)™ *Respect is where it's at!*

(aHa!)™ *Put a lid on your ego!*

(aHa!)™ *Grow people!*

(aHa!)™ *Step aside!*

(aHa!)™ *"E R R" your way to success!*

(aHa!)™ *Duh! Write it down!*

(aHa!)™ *Do the right thing, no matter what!*

(aHa!)™ *Create the adventure!*

(aHa!)™ *Better TRUSTED than busted!*

EPILOGUE

How much you know and apply measures how far you go!

You've just been through some straight forward common sense *leadership principles* shared here from first hand *in-the-trenches* experiences. You must always strive to be a perpetual student, because it *gains you the edge.* The progress of the next five years of your life will be determined by the books you read, the continuing education you seek and the people you associate with. This book was designed to help you in that process.

Focus on *gaining the edge* across the board. You'll *gain the edge* faster by becoming just 1% better in 100 areas rather than trying to be 100% better in just one area.

Keep this book handy as a ready reference. Refer back to it <u>frequently</u> when situations arise that are addressed here. Always remember:

> **It's not the static possession of knowledge, but the dynamic flow that makes you valuable; not just job knowledge, but especially knowing how to manage, motivate and lead people.**

You are to be commended for taking this vital step to improve your leadership skills. You now have the tools to move forward to <u>change</u> your life and that of others. ❑

ABOUT THE AUTHORS

The authors are founders of Real Leaders Institute, LLC, a leadership information, training and education organization.

Len Fuchs is a retired United States Marine Corps Colonel with over 3,000 hours of flight time in tactical fighters. In the military Len held a number of key leadership positions including squadron commanding officer, U.S. Government "Drug Czar" in South America and program manager in the Global Positioning Satellite System (GPS). After his military career, Len became Senior Vice President of the Government Division of Franklin Covey Company providing time management organizing products. He then went on to found an executive leadership training company. His mission: ***"Change lives through ethical leadership training."***

Len Fuchs (L) during air control liaison duty in Vietnam in 1971 with South Korean counterpart, showing that leadership is an international language.

John Nicholas has held executive positions with Fortune 500 and NYSE companies including IBM and the former investment banking firm of F.I. duPont & Company. He became an entrepreneur and founded manufacturing, real estate investment and consulting firms which included international representation.

John is a former U.S. Navy officer with service aboard a guided missile cruiser. He holds a degree in Sociology and was listed in past editions of Who's Who in Professional Speaking.

In 2003 he retired from a national home building company in which he was the charter member of the corporate university development team. His training and education topics were leadership, management, interpersonal skills, negotiation, delegation and empowerment. He has since published articles in those areas which have had wide circulation. His mission: ***"Set an example of trust, integrity and ethics in leadership training."***

Another leadership source

www.ThoughtsWhileShaving.com
Subscribed to by leaders from major coporations to the Pentagon. Founded by Len Fuchs, author of *Thoughts While Shaving, Volume I.*

A free newsletter with 5 -6 short leadership common sense sayings sent out weekly, such as: *"Leaders don't get tied up in endless strategy meetings looking for the perfect solution."*

By accessing the above site you can be certain your privacy will be respected.

Services Available

Len Fuchs and John Nicholas conduct leadership training programs covering leadership, performance management, interpersonal skills, delegation, empowerment and vision development implementation. Further, they offer customized coaching and mentoring.

Contact Information:

Len Fuchs & John Nicholas

Real Leaders Institute, LLC

P.O. Box 2557

Gilbert, AZ 85299

USA

Telephone/fax: 480.219.5509

email: support@LeaderNowWhat.com

Website: www.LeaderNowWhat.com

www.ingramcontent.com/pod-product-compliance
Lightning Source LLC
Chambersburg PA
CBHW070249190526
45169CB00001B/349